Nigerian Gems

Expatriate Tales of Adventure

Nigerian Gems

Expatriate Tales of Adventure

Compiled and edited by Jo Demmer and Gail Collins
Design and Layout by Els Van Limberghen

All proceeds support Nigerian children's education
Published by Ishahayi Beach School Foundation

e-mail: ishahayibeachschoolfoundation@yahoo.co.uk
website: www.nigeriangems.org

ISBN 978-066-886-1

Printed by Simon Printers Limited
Plot 124 Oyadiran Estate, Sabo, Yaba, Lagos, Nigeria

Invitation

From Jo Demmer and Gail Collins

We would like to take you by the hand and show you the streets of Lagos - crowded, noisy and in a state of disrepair. Okada drivers dodge between the cars with inches to spare in apparent disregard for anyone's safety including their own. Car horns blow for every reason but affect little change.

Now, climb into our boat, and we'll escort you up Five Mile Creek and out to Ishahayi Beach - secluded, quiet, beautiful and incredibly poor. It is a weekday, so we watch the villagers cast enormous fishing nets, then work together to haul them back to the shore. In this primitive but time-honoured way, their catch for the day will be the village's sole source of income.

Let's stop by Ishahayi Beach School, and we'll introduce you to Lady Evans Dorcas Salami, the Nigerian missionary who established and runs the village school. She proudly shows us the school where she has invested countless hours for little or no pay over the past five years. Lady Salami's home is nearby, a 2.5 m by 2 m shack with a bed made of boards and no mattress. We see you are moved, as we were, by the extreme devotion of this amazing woman.

The school tour does not take long - one small, wooden hut housing 70 students. Yes, it's charming here by the sea under palm trees, but the roof leaks on the sand floor and there is nowhere to store school supplies, if they had any. And what use is charm in a world where high school is mandatory for employment, university degrees are essential for higher-paying jobs and post-graduate studies are standard for most senior jobs?

Fishing boat, Ishahayi Beach. Photo by Gail Collins

Lady Salami. Photo by Ben Wilkins

By now, word has spread that there are visitors at the school and 10 to 15 children have come to see what is happening. They are eager and smiling. In threadbare clothes and bare feet, they seat us on a wooden bench. They clap, stomp and sing for us in cheerfulness and innocence. Surrounded by these beautiful children, you would understand our compulsion to ensure them a chance for the future. An education encourages self-reliance and independence. An education brings hope.

Where are you from? In Australia or the States where we come from, education is considered a birthright. It is outlawed to withdraw a child from school before the age of 16. In Nigeria, education is still a privilege. We aim to extend this privilege to all the children of Ishahayi Beach. This book has been written, edited and designed entirely by volunteers. Our only cost was printing for which we received sponsorship. All proceeds will go directly to support the Ishahayi Beach school.

We wish we could bring you here. Who hasn't ever had a wild thought of Africa? In *Nigerian Gems*, through our words and photographs, you will glimpse traffic, beaches, markets, festivals, local heroes, and more that comprises this fascinating and complex country, Nigeria.

Where Our Stories Take Place

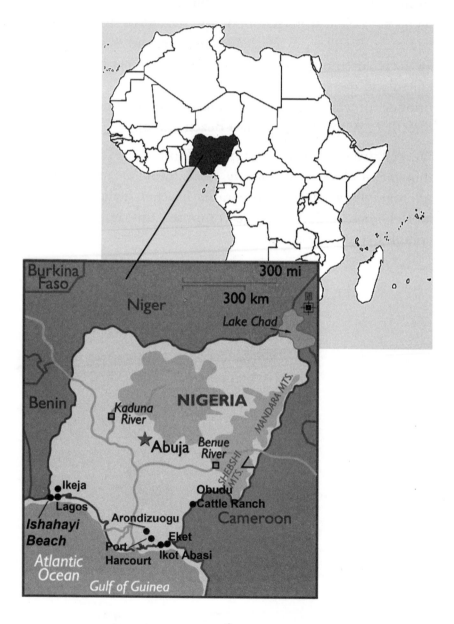

Table of Contents

A Single Man Cannot Build a House

Acknowledgements

Australian Jo Demmer sat in the rough wooden hut deep in conversation with the school founder, Lady Salami. Jo asked, "What does the school need?" Thinking along the lines of exercise books and pencils, she was caught off guard as Lady Salami quietly said, "We would like a roof for our school. This one leaks, and during the rainy season, we are wet." Jo looked around the ramshackle, reed structure with hewn benches, a chalkboard, a basket of letter and number blocks, but little else and said, "You will need to give me some time for that one." Jo trudged through the sand under the dazzling African sunshine back to the shore where her family relaxed and played at their company beach hut. Palm trees rustled from the ocean breeze and her thoughts stayed on the children of the Ishahayi Beach Light Nursery & Primary School.

Sitting around the pool of her compound in Lagos, Jo chatted with friends who had recently returned from luxurious, refreshing summers in their home countries. She had already tried out the idea on her husband, but for the first time, she voiced her plan in public, "I'd like to write a book. A book of stories about what it's like to be a foreigner living in Nigeria. The profits from sales can be used to help pay for school repairs and supplies out at Ishahayi Beach." But Jo knew the money would be long in coming from the sale of a book that had not yet been written. Still, there was enthusiasm to help, and she teamed an international collection of women to form the Ishahayi Beach School Foundation (IBSF).

Jared Eckert, a ninth grader, needed a project to earn his Eagle

12

Old schoolhouse, Ishahayi Beach.
Photo by Jared Eckert

Working on new schoolhouse,
Ishahayi Beach.
Photo by Jo Demmer

New schoolhouse, Ishahayi Beach,
before project. Photo by Jo Demmer

Scout rank, and decided to help IBSF organize the completion of a school building that stood next to the leaky hut. The foundation had previously been poured and a few rows of concrete blocks laid, but there was a long way to go, and they needed sponsors to guarantee the project. The American Women's Club (AWC) was calling to fund one-off capital projects for worthy charities. Presented with building quotes and moving photographs, the AWC readily granted one million naira to complete the schoolhouse. In three months it was built, lead by a local contractor, Benjamin Solomon, and crew. Jared organized work days with Boy Scout Troop #803 and associated families, who mixed concrete and painted inside and out the soft hues of a beach sunset.

IBSF, assisted by Kathy and Jeff Eckert, Jared's parents, compiled a contact list of companies and community groups. IBSF then continued the fundraising. Mobil Producing Nigeria, operator of the NNPC/MPN Joint Venture, gave a significant contribution, Miabo devoted a portion of her local café sales to IBSF and hosted an art exhibition to support the cause, the Lagos Yacht Club donated funds from a charity event, Shell's community also gave a generous donation and Chevron helped out with printing costs. The project felt graced from the start. When people heard members talk about the school at clubs, dinner parties and at coffees, needs were enthusiastically met.

The talents and contacts of IBSF members were as varied as the nationalities - Michelle Ukoh, an American school principal, designed the curriculum and lesson plans, and enlisted the support of Nigerian Lawyer O. A. Faboro, Esq. on issues of Nigerian law; Australian Raelene Dinnick handled accounting while her husband, Peter, advised on legal issues; Ilonka Hoffmanns made significant inroads fundraising through groups in Lagos and in her home country of Holland; Dutch Geke Buiten replaced Ilonka after her return to Holland; American Shelley Fazzino organized school furniture requirements; Fabienne Zivny of France used her marketing background to assist Nigerian Miabo in organising an art exhibition; Australian Robyn Fisher and American Angela Stevens ensured that all our sponsors were thanked appropriately; and Australian Lindy Edwards managed the book launch and marketing.

Behind these active work scenes, the book project moved forward. The school would need regular income for ongoing costs, and steady book sales could provide that. Jo asked American Gail Collins to help write and edit the book. Gail was beginning to write freelance for magazines and understood the dedication and work of publishing. She thought that Jo dreamed big, and figured she had no idea what the process would entail. But she said yes and the vision grew.

They put out the call for submissions from all ages and all nationalities for stories written in English and for photographs. Promotional flyers and presentations were made to the American International School of Lagos (AISL) and various companies and clubs in Lagos about IBSF to create enthusiasm for the project. The stories rolled in. Forty-three contributors hail from a host of countries - Peru, USA, Canada, Australia, Malaysia, England, Holland and Nigeria - with overseas experience in Indonesia, China, Angola, Germany, Qatar, Saudi Arabia and more.

Visual images of traffic, people and places brought their adventures and daily routines to life. Taking photographs of

Nigerians proved an education for both photographer and subject. Some Nigerians believe that taking their photograph takes away a part of their soul. By showing them instant digital images the camera's purpose was revealed, reassuring and delighting them. Closer contact with Nigerian daily life, even through a camera lens, was an eye-opening reality check for the expats.

The editors looked for a seal of approval on the book from professional writing circles. Tapping into serendipity, Jo invited Australian children's author, Richard Tulloch, to visit the Ishahayi School with them during his tour of Africa. Screenwriter for the popular "Bananas in Pyjamas," Richard appeals to youngsters to create stories, and he wrote of his travels in Nigeria for the book. A couple of freelance writers added a comedic flavor with other stories, and the caliber of entertainment and writing edged up.

Writing and printing a book for the first time is a steep learning curve. Jo and Gail spent hundreds of hours honing work and dialoguing with authors. They researched travel writing and publishing, applied for funding and asked for discounts. And help. Proof readers, Sara Dobbs, Judy Anderson and Martha Peterson, plowed through all the pieces for continuity, comprehension and referred to Craig Curry for the final say on grammar. Contributions of time and talent also made the final steps of formatting the book possible through graphic designer, Els Van Limberghen from Belgium. Els added her expertise to turn the vision into the pages of a real book.

Nigerians were gracious hosts and offered inspiration for these stories. Colleagues, stewards, drivers, nannies, cooks, street vendors, princes, okada drivers, police and guards provided the

New schoolhouse,
Ishahayi Beach.
Photo by Katrina Head

Jared Eckert and
Lady Salami with
school children.
Photo by Jeff Eckert

authors with fun, humour, sometimes fear and always learning. In particular, Joseph Dahunsi and Happiness Udoh acted as Nigerian consultants for communication between expats and Nigerians and checking book contents for authenticity.

Throughout, it was the men behind the women who allowed the project, which began as a tentative suggestion needing support, to become the 200-page volume, *Nigerian Gems*. Andrew Barton and Jim Collins kept morale high, offered suggestions, listened to endless discussions about people and their work, let their wives rant in frustration, soothed their brain meltdowns, gave in to daily editing sessions that dragged through lunch, dinner and sometimes into the night and mocked up the first cover with smiling children to assure them it was a wonderful idea. They made hard work into fun.

Nigerian Gems is a community project in every way. The book reflects the expat community living within the local community. It took a community to write it and publish it, and a community will buy it, read it, and pass it on to lift up still another community. Its stories are gems about this place and about the people filling its pages. Thank you to all the gems who made this book possible.

Forward to the Reprint

By Jo Demmer

Nearly three years have passed since the first edition of *Nigerian Gems* was published. Five thousand copies have been printed and demand is still strong, so we are going back to print. Many wonderful things have happened in those three years, all of which improve the level of education in Ishahayi Beach and its surrounding areas.

Ishahayi Beach School Foundation (IBSF) has evolved and thrived. While I am the only original member still in Lagos, new people have joined the team with fresh enthusiasm and drive.

Mural designed by Eugene Chime on new school building.
Photo by Gerry Aroozoo

Our current members include: Gerry Aroozoo (our new Chairperson), Rachel Bassett, Amy Cope-Gibbs, Shelly Foster, Hilde Gjervik, John Guise, Naz Henham, Teresa Sabatini and Jane Wood. I would like to acknowledge the great contributions of all our members: the original members listed in "A Single Man Cannot Build a House," our current members and some who have come and gone in between, including Angela Barletta, Sophie Batchelor, Sara Dobbs and Liz Smith.

Lady Salami is still the guiding beacon at the school. Replete with 5 other teachers and 120 students, the school is abuzz with action. Benjamin Solomon consistently does an excellent job on our building projects. After the first one-room building, we provided:

- a six-room building to provide separate classrooms for the various grade levels

- a large verandah across the front of classrooms to give an outside sheltered area

- a new well and pump

- a toilet block with 3 lavatories and a shower (this is the only running shower for miles around)

- school desks, benches, teachers desks and book-shelves

- a full curriculum of school books

- a computer

- ongoing support to the school

New verandah for classroom building at Ishahayi Beach.
Photo by John Guise.

Toilet block under construction at Ishahayi Beach.
Photo by John Guise.

New well, classrooms & toiletblock
at Ishahayi Beach.
Photo by John Guise.

Computer room
at Ishahayi Beach.
Photo by John Guise.

When we reached this stage, we wanted to broaden the scope of IBSF and looked for other nearby schools needing help. The children who complete grade 6 at Ishahayi Beach can further their education at Ikare Junior Grammar School. After visiting this school and spending time building trust and rapport with the school teachers and villagers, we decided to extend our work there. We raised money to build three classrooms and are now improving three more. Much more work is still needed at this school, which, over time, we hope to accomplish. As the foundation grows, we stand ready to venture into three other schools in the region.

Local organisations have supported IBSF and, whether providing funds to print Nigerian Gems, donating money for building projects or buying school books and furniture, they have given generously and with a good heart. Mobil Producing Nigeria, Chevron, Lagos Yacht Club, Small World (the Australian and New Zealand team from 2006, Australian team 2007 and Scandinavian team 2008), American Women's Club Lagos (AWC), MTN and American International School Lagos (AISL) have all helped our cause. A number of individuals have also given private donations, some from as far away as the USA and Australia. Funds from books sales have been used for ongoing expenses at Ishahayi Beach School and for some parts of our building projects. Reprint sales will be used predominantly for Ishahayi Beach School, but may be also used for other schools in the region.

To keep our readers informed, we have created a website, www.nigeriangems.org. One question that has been asked

Students from Ikare with books
donated by AISL.
Photo by John Guise.

Ikare classroom before building.
Photo by John Guise.

New classrooms at Ikare.
Photo by John Guise.

Students at Ikare.
Photo by Naz Henman.

many times is whether we are going to write Nigerian Gems 2. When the time is right, this may take place, but at the moment we are not making that commitment. If this decision is made, notice of it will be advertised on our website, so keep watching.

Thank you for buying this book. At the end of the day, this is all about children and education. Watching bright, young faces glow with enthusiasm as they learn and seeing teachers' pride in their students and classrooms is a joy. To sustain and improve this level of education is our hope and plan.

Editors' Note

Nigerian Gems is a collection of stories written by expatriates about their adventures in Nigeria. We share our lives and promote Nigeria to family and friends, armchair travelers, charity supporters and those considering a move here. Aiming for good-will, we emphasize the positive aspects of life in Nigeria. The complete accounting must include some unsettling truths of residing in a country with mass poverty, but we would like outsiders to witness that there is more to Nigeria than headlines plugging riots and corruption. We highlight the friendliness and warmth of Nigerians, the fascinating and different culture, and we chuckle at our struggles to create a home in a foreign land.

One of the greatest joys and challenges of working on this book was having an international authorship (eight countries of origin) and readership. Early in the project, we faced the quandary of whether to write in British or American English. Naturally, Gail rooted for American and Jo cheered for British. Already aware that there were differences in spelling and expressions, as the book progressed, we also unearthed differences in grammar. For example, Americans put a period after Mr. and Mrs. whereas

British English writers prefer Mr and Mrs without a full stop.

Working hard to polish the gems of stories we had been given, we strove to maintain the voice of each author. For several of our authors, English is their second language and we enjoyed the idiosyncrasies of their language. So, in order to maintain authenticity, we decided to use the English of the author. You will notice differences in spelling and some aspects of grammar between pieces. A glossary has been placed at the back of the book to explain colloquial terms instead of interrupting the flow of the text. We hope you enjoy this diversity as much as we have and that our gems sparkle to their best effect.

Nigeria's visual and private landscape shaped the narrators of *Nigerian Gems* by confirming their distinct differences while laying bare the humbling common ground between people. We immersed ourselves in a place we knew little or nothing about and wrote of our journey, so others can accompany us into the active Africa we call home.

First Impressions

Gems. Photo by Els Van Limberghen
Lizard. Photo by Ilonka Hoffmanns
Child carrying baby. Photo by Bob Griffiths
A van full. Photo by Els Van Limberghen

Arrival In Africa

By Kathy Eckert

You are welcome! This typical Nigerian greeting can mean welcome, hello, good day and more. It's what we heard when we arrived safely, albeit tired, in this place.

I had a range of immense emotions over the weeks leading up to our move to Lagos. Upon arriving, I vacillated between jumping for joy and crying from enormous relief that after five months of planning - shopping, packing, paperwork, shots and sad goodbyes - we finally did get here.

I left with my three children for Houston's airport in mid-August in two taxivans packed with seven footlockers, eleven suitcases, three backpacks and one totebag. My husband, Jeff, was already in Lagos. When people questioned our load, we answered, "Yes, we're staying for more than a weekend, and yes, basically we are going to Timbuktu." Even with a three-and-a-half-hour head start, we barely made it onboard our flight before the doors closed. Now we could breathe a sigh of relief because there was nothing else to do for the next eleven-plus hours, except rest and relax. And I needed it.

The flight to London was comfortable thanks to Business Class accommodation - our seats reclined into beds - so we managed four hours of sleep before landing at 10 am (4 am by our body clocks). We planned this stopover to see the sites and break up our journey before heading on to Lagos. After checking every case into Left Luggage, we feigned consciousness, our heads nodding as we toured London by Underground, double-decker bus and boat. Probably, the only thing my kids will remember about Britain is the drunk on the subway who wet himself - a teaching moment on the evils of alcohol!

The next day at Heathrow, we retraced our steps, collected our baggage, checked it in and made our way to the gate marked "Lagos" - standing room only. Ryan quickly pointed out, "Mom, do you realize we're the only white people here?" So began our assimilation as a minority. Soon, three other expat families joined us and the kids made friends and disappeared with them for the entire flight to Africa. Two of the families turned out to be neighbors in our compound.

I was awestruck flying over Northern Africa. Watching the dunes of the Sahara give way to red, cracked mud, slowly yielding to grassy fields, and finally, the lush tropics of West Africa was incredible. Being used to the uniform pastures and farms of the American Midwest, this irregular terrain excited me, including a tree which looked like broccoli from the air.

Before landing, I checked that the kids had filled their water bottles, used the restroom, and understood my 25th lecture about staying next to me at all times. To my surprise, the airport was not a corrugated, open-air metal shack, but fairly modern. Jeff was not allowed into the airport, but left to wait behind a fence with mobs of local people, however, he had the foresight to hire an expediter to help us through Immigration and Baggage. After an eternity, and umpteen offers to help me for a dash, we made it through Customs with all our bags and without being stopped - God was in that, NO doubt.

Outside, the hundreds of jostling people caused confusion and chaos. Where were our security guys in red jumpsuits? Where were my sons? Lugging a suitcase through the throng, would my daughter be lost, stolen or trampled? Where was Jeff? And then, I saw our security team and two white faces in the crowd - one was Jeff's! Soon, we were in his arms, and after three and a half hours, including a bus ride escorted by vehicles with armed guards, we were in our new home. The kids were ecstatic, but exhausted, so we hardly noticed our rock-hard beds. But the next day, we noticed everything - our beds and all the things that made up our new life.

Power Cuts

By Christine Laurenssen

Before moving to Lagos, I had heard about the frequent power-cuts, however, I didn't really expect to experience my first blackout at the airport. Whilst I waited amidst the chaos of raucous children, baggage trolleys and porters manhandling people's belongings, the entire airport suddenly plunged into complete and utter darkness. After a bit of screaming and howling from those stranded in the baggage claim area, (one can only assume they were afraid of the dark) a guy turned on a Mini Maglite to illuminate the hall filled with about 300 people. For five minutes we waited by the light of this one torch until the generator finally kicked in.

Since then, I experience approximately two power cuts a day at the office in Ikeja with another one thrown in for good measure at night in Lekki. It's an incredibly strange feeling, while talking to a client, to suddenly plunge into two minutes of total blackness, until the generator kicks in. It gives me the giggles but everyone else just carries on regardless.

Beer and Gum

By Mike Garbarini

In 1987, I came to Nigeria for the first time to introduce in-house computer mapping capability to the oil patch. Pre-trip advice from working friends suggested: don't listen to Medical about all those shots and malaria pills, book your own travel flying via Rio to Lagos, and take all of your equipment with you on the plane, except ship those enormous plotters. One friend gave me the only wary warning saying, "Never take a taxi in Lagos."

Armed with all this great advice, the Rio Airport Authorities immediately hung me up under house arrest for three days in the terminal building. I slept with my 37 boxes of equipment due to lack of a visitor's visa and inherent plane delays becoming bored and bedraggled.

Finally in Lagos, I found Customs to be part mob scene, riot and shakedown. A steady stream of officials demanded "import duty" from me, and I settled with each group of them, pleased to move on to the next, hoping to find Baggage Claim. There I witnessed strangers busily carrying off my boxes.

Some boys were hanging around nearby, so I offered them money and formed my own safari/caravan porter crew... to where? To the sidewalk, as it turned out, doing my best to keep my porters from wandering away or opening boxes. Remembering the admonition, "Never take a taxi in Lagos," I approached a line of people who were boarding a private bus. I begged the man holding a company sign who was clearly coordinating their arrival, "Please have pity on me." The Samaritan secured six taxis for me and negotiated payment in advance. I'd lost some ground already and loaded only 32 boxes into the cars.

The drivers were kind enough to dump my boxes out at the curb of the office building before rushing away. People standing there helped me haul the boxes up the steps and into the lobby. Now there were 31, and I utilized every one of them to block hall traffic to the elevator on the Sixth Floor until my boss showed up an hour later. He stood downwind as I gave him the story before he quickly said, "You paid too much at Customs. Welcome to Nigeria! Get some rest and a bath."

At the staff house, I found even that endeavor a challenge, but I was greeted with welcoming gifts such as a roll of toilet paper and a light bulb for my room. After showering, I covered myself with insect repellent, pulled the covers completely over my head, and as the sound of mosquitoes lulled me to sleep, I thought about the malaria tablets I'd been told not to bother with.

Our team digitized over 50 maps during my training session in Lagos, but could make no hard copies. The plotter and its spare had arrived weeks before my trip, but one of the machines had only been retrieved after a "brief" exposure to rain. When the plotter dried out, we fired her up, and she gave a satisfying hum as the pen raced back and forth across the paper during the initialization sequence. Then it locked up. There were no error messages... it just didn't work. We called Technical Assistance in the US, and the nice gentleman on the phone diagnosed the problem rather quickly - a piece of reflecting foil was missing completely on one end of the plotter and curled up into a wad on the other. "No problem," said the technician, "Just give me an address, and I'll send over a repairman." We had a good laugh, and of course, they didn't send a repairman or a do-it-yourself repair kit. It was up to us.

So, on my last day planned in the office, we still could not make hard copies of our work, and it was a somber departure dinner. We recognized the progress made and cheered ourselves gradually as we consumed a number of those tall Nigerian beers. As I sat peeling the label off my beer bottle, a habit from college, it struck me that we could use the foil label for replacement parts on the plotter. Like all ideas one has when drinking, it sounded pretty good at the time, "A bit of glue and foil; we'll be just fine!" A few more beers secured our plan.

In the "cold grey light of dawn" as the country song goes, we arrived at the office without any beer labels to solve our world's problems, just a beer headache. We did, however, manage to peel the foil off a Juicy Fruit gum wrapper and superglue it to the plotter. It worked for over a year.

Office Improvements

By Jack Carter

In July 1988, two colleagues and I were assigned to meet face to face with technical users in Nigeria to determine how we could improve upstream computing. We arrived in Lagos on a late night flight, and I recalled the advice of a fellow traveler as I approached Immigration, "Don't take the escalator." So, I didn't. I learned why. The escalator delivered passengers down into a sea of humanity jammed at Immigration. Those mechanical stairs kept pushing people into an area where there was nowhere to go. They simply could not get off! Two or three men with bags in each hand rode the thing taking backward steps in time trying not to fall off or be conveyed into the crowd.

We reported to the Bookshop House office to start work looking for opportunities to improve computing for technologists. As we toured the building, we noticed a way to help immediately. The senior management administrators, short of cabinet space, filed their floppy disks in envelopes, then pinned them to their cubicle walls. Instead of putting the pin through the hole in the middle of the 5-1/4" floppy, or in the envelope area beyond the disk, they were happily slicing the pin right through the media. We shared this tip with an administrator, and she excitedly called others to tell them of the new procedure and solution to why they couldn't read their floppies after "filing" them.

Our visit was great. The folks we met were terrific, the hospitality was good, and we learned a lot about the needs of a remote office.

Cat's Papers

By Judy Anderson

As newcomers arriving through Murtala Mohammed Airport, we had our cat in a pet carrier, complete with all the proper papers. I had spent hours on the documents and with the veterinarian in the U.S. to ensure nothing could go wrong upon our entry.

After we collected all of our baggage, including the cat, we were stopped by a uniformed official, asking about the animal. I was confident I had covered all the bases, so I handed him the file. My confidence eroded quickly as the official took quite a long time perusing it. After many minutes, another uniformed man came over, looked over the first man's shoulder, then gently took the papers out of his hands. Turning the documents right side up, he handed them back. And we still had to pay a dash!

The Ducky Potty Man

By Richard Tulloch

I was new to Nigeria. I'd just arrived in Lagos that morning, less than an hour earlier. But as soon as I caught the vendor's eye through the car window I knew I'd made a mistake. I'd shown a flicker of interest in what he was selling and now he expected me to buy it - a toddler's ducky potty.

I didn't mean to stare. I know that in these potentially awkward circumstances it's best to hide behind sunglasses and feign blindness, or speak loudly into a cell phone so you look like a busy man on a mission. After several stints in Asia and four whole weeks in Africa, I was an old hand at smiling politely and brushing away zebra necklaces and phone cards and Ladysmith Black Mambazo CDs and "Rolex" watches as if they were troublesome flies.

But this was new to me - a young man in a "go-slow" trying to sell ducky potties to passing motorists. I mean, when you're caught in a traffic jam, it's possible that you might develop the need for a bottle of cool water, or an orange, or a bag of nuts, or a newspaper, or even a phone card if you have to let someone know that at this rate you won't make it to the office for another five hours, so you've decided to go and play golf instead. It seems unlikely that you'd suddenly experience an overwhelming urge to buy a ducky potty.

Who is this man? I wondered. What made him decide to sell potties by the roadside? Are they his potties, or is he an agent for someone who's found a large batch of toilet items fallen off the back of a truck, and who now needs help to offload them? How many potties does he sell in a day? In a year? How much profit margin is there in selling a potty? When he was a kid, did he aspire to be a potty vendor when he grew up? Do his parents talk proudly about "our son who's in Lagos doing something very big in potties?" Is he hoping this potty business will be a temporary phase in his career; something to tide him over in hard times until a more glamorous job turns up? Is he maybe an actor between engagements, or a student putting himself through medical college?

The point is, the ducky potty man has no choice. If he could do anything else in life, he wouldn't choose to stand in the heat and the traffic fumes, hoping against hope that the next car to inch past might just want a ducky potty. If he had any choice at all in what he could sell, he'd go for something with a bit more commercial oomph than ducky potties.

We fill our lives planning what we'd like to do, where we'd like our careers to take us, what our children will be when they grow up, deciding where to go on our next holiday. Such decisions cannot possibly be a part of the ducky potty man's world. And he represents most of the world's population.

I raised my eyebrows at him, trying to indicate amused incredulity that he might think a big grown up boy like me might still need a potty. He put on his best pleading expression. I shrugged. I didn't even have any local currency yet. The ducky potty man gave up, grinned broadly and gave me a cheerful wave. I had to admire him. If I had to swap places with him, I don't think I'd be grinning and waving very often.

The car crept away from him, and his place at the car window was taken in turn by vendors selling dog leashes, magazines and dartboards. "American International School," said my driver, pointing into the middle distance to a group of nondescript buildings surrounded by other groups of nondescript buildings.

"How long until we get there?" I asked.

"Depend on traffic," he said, "we have to take long way round, then come back. This street, only one way. Maybe half hour."

The cars in front were still barely moving. My plane out of Nairobi had been cancelled the day before and I'd been awake all night waiting for the next flight to leave. I was expecting to work that afternoon, so I'd boosted my consciousness with a few cups of coffee on the plane. Now the third and fourth cups were working their way to my bladder. There was nowhere for the driver to pull over. We were in the middle lane of a highway in a built-up area, maybe even within sight of kids and parents and teachers at the school where I'd be working for the next week. I wished I'd bought a ducky potty.

Selling rat poison.
Photo by
Charlie Fazzino

Lost In Translation

By Sara Dobbs

I had reservations about moving to Lagos, Nigeria and knew it had the potential to be a tough assignment. But I took comfort knowing that I'd have the luxury of experiencing a vibrant foreign culture, without the struggle of learning a new language. Unlike its French-speaking neighbors, Nigeria's colonial history determined that English would be the lingua franca making it relatively easy for American expatriates. I only needed to learn a few Yoruba greetings and phrases at my leisure, brush-up on a few British terms (boot, windscreen, jumper, etc...) and develop an ear for the local vernacular. I was confident that communication would be a snap.

One week after arriving, I felt bombarded with information, decisions and new smells. I was dizzy from a combination of jet lag and sensory overload, and it wasn't as easy to understand the local dialect or accent as I'd first anticipated. Ordinarily an independent person, I surrendered to reliance on household staff, especially my driver. Pious was a new and somewhat inexperienced driver - eager to work, eager to please and not too set in his ways. He was smart, articulate, and I could understand his English perfectly. The first few days went well. Then one morning, Pious was late for work. I was at first puzzled and then, disappointed. As 20 minutes turned into 30, I became increasingly irritated. Wasn't he taking this job seriously? Why would he have such a blatant disregard for my schedule? Something must have happened, and his excuse had better be good.

Finally, Pious showed up slightly out of breath and apologetic. "What happened this morning?" I asked in my best "employer" voice. With a heavy sigh and a look of resignation, he stated matter-of-factly, "There was a big hold up on the expressway." "A hold up?" Shock must have been evident on my face. Visions of masked gunmen terrorizing a yellow bus flooded my mind, and I launched a barrage of questions: "A hold up? Oh-my-gosh, was anyone hurt? Did they take your money? Did anyone call the police? Did the police arrive? Are you all right?" I wanted a detailed account, but instead, Pious didn't seem to want to talk about it. He just looked at me quizzically and assured me that he was O.K. Respecting his privacy, I didn't press the issue.

While Pious looked remarkably calm and composed, I, on the other hand, was feeling more distraught by the minute. My thoughts swirled: "A hold up... I can't believe it... in broad daylight on the expressway... I was warned about crime before moving to Lagos, but this was so brazen." I asked Pious if he wanted something to drink and told him to take the rest of the morning off. He said he was fine, declined the offer to go home and set about washing the car. I was genuinely amazed how well he was coping and impressed with his professionalism. Here was a driver I could depend on in a time of crisis. I reasoned that instead of displaying his emotions, he accepted that this was life in Lagos, and crime simply went with the territory.

I relayed the news to my husband at lunchtime and spoke to a few other people that day, but no one else had heard any details. I was surprised that the story hadn't spread and figured that the gunmen must have escaped before the police could make any arrests.

A few days later, I was paging through "Lagos Easy Access the Guidebook" trying to soak up as much information on Nigeria as I could. Studying "Lagosian Words & Phrases," I discovered that "419" was the term for fraud, and "chop" was a meal. Suddenly, there it was, staring me in the face: the term "hold up!" I laughed so hard I nearly cried. "Hold up," like "go-slow," simply meant traffic jam.

Pious' unwavering composure that day and his confused look at my overwrought state now made perfect sense. I thought about explaining myself, but where would I begin? I tried out different approaches in my mind: "You see, in the U.S. a 'hold up' is like 'stick 'em up,' you know, a robbery? In the movies?" It was futile. Effective communication would take a lot more effort on my part, beginning with simple words and phrases. I suppose I should have broached the subject of traffic jams with Pious, but I couldn't bear the thought of admitting that I was so ignorant about everyday language in Nigeria. Instead, I decided never to mention the "hold up" again with him, or anyone else.

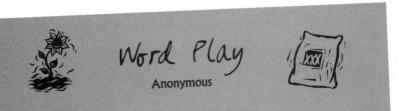

Word Play

Anonymous

I sent out my driver to buy flowers and he came back with a bag of flour. Another day, craving some chocolate, I sent him for a Kit Kat. He returned with Kitty Kat Food.

Settling In
By Kim Davis

I arrived in Lagos two and half weeks ago and have started to venture past the confines of my compound walls. One result is always the same: I return home hot and sweaty!

Yesterday, I went with 12 ladies and an entourage of police (we are given security whenever we leave Lekki and Victoria Island) to buy fabric at Balagun market in the heart of Lagos Island. It had rained so hard that the ground was one big mud puddle. After sloshing past trays of indiscernible meat parts, giant snails, dried fish, undergarments and toiletries, we arrived at the fabric stalls. Between 75 and 100 stalls stood in rows two feet apart. Two-way pedestrian traffic negotiated these tiny passages, so while trying to make sense of the barrage of patterns and colors before me, I dodged women carrying two-foot-wide trays of wares on their heads, guys with wheel barrows full of cinder blocks and an assortment of other busy people barreling past. I was jostled and bumped as people forced their way through the crowd.

Abeokuta Market. Photo by Judy Anderson

Like me, most of my group was overwhelmed with the heat, human traffic and endless meters of loud fabric, so we resorted to quick purchases. However, there were two die-hard, old hands who got into the spirit of the whole adventure and continued to haggle and bargain their way through the 100 stalls. While waiting for the group to reassemble, I bought apples, green peppers, soap and a case of bottled water (which the seller carried to my car on her head). It was a productive 10 minutes.

I was shocked when I returned to the parking lot and found my car sandwiched in on all sides by other vehicles. The prospects of a speedy departure appeared grim. Then, before I knew what was happening, my driver, Lawrence, with the help of some other drivers in the parking lot began pushing cars out of the way. They literally pushed the cars as though they were pieces in a board game until there was space for us to get out. Finally out of the parking lot, Lawrence and I fought our way through downtown Lagos, bumper to bumper.

Today, in a revolt against the fish man who sells astronomically priced fish in our compound, I decided to venture out to find seafood at the source. Lawrence, Maria (our Argentine maid who came to Lagos with us) and I headed out to Epe about an hour away. The drive was quite relaxed, with less development and a lush landscape of palm trees and shrubs. My car sounds an alarm at any speed over 90 km (54mph), so we drove slowly on an almost empty highway. It felt like a breath of fresh air leaving the congestion of the city behind.

At the Epe fish market, we were obliged to hire two ladies as our "escorts." They led us to the fisherman's catches... WOW!... masses of fish, shrimp, crabs, and even a couple of crocodiles for sale. Most were still breathing and flopping around, so there was no doubt that they were fresh! The first five to ten minutes were interesting, until the saleswomen swooped in and ended the fun. Ten women surrounded us holding fish by the tail and swinging them in our faces shouting, "Buy this fish Madame!" At one point I shouted back, "Quit yelling at me! I can't think!"

As the women proceeded with the selling ritual, Maria and I tried to escape by inching further and further backwards. Before I knew it, we were on the edge of a concrete pier with nowhere to go but into the water. I thought we would end up taking a swim to elude the fish women. Bargaining can be torture and at some point I don't care what it costs, I just want it to be over. So finally, with severe pressure to buy or take a swim, I haggled half-heartedly and made a deal for a five-kilo shiny nose. One of my escorts, with her gorgeous baby strapped to her back, grabbed the fish by its tail and headed towards the car. Now that I'd made a purchase, the saleswomen backed off. On my way out, I made another speedier deal for a whole tray of croaker - a type of white fish.

My escorts, fish in tow, were now heading away from my car. Alarmed, I questioned Lawrence, and he informed me that they intended to clean the fish - that was part of their job. There was no way I was going to let them clean my fish with their dirty knife and questionable water. I quickly told Lawrence to take the fish away from them and put it in the car. The ladies watched perplexed as he tried to bend the big shiny nose to fit into my little cooler-bag. By now I'd had more than enough and I said, "Hurry, let's get out of here." Of course the escort fee was the same with or without the fish cleaning! After paying someone else to get out of the parking lot, Maria and I breathed big sighs of relief and laughed incredulously as we pulled away. All this for cheaper fish! Afterwards, Lawrence mentioned that we had not been over to the part of the market where they sell "bush meat," such as monkeys. I think that would have done me in!

On our way home, I decided to show Maria the beach where some of my friends have beach huts. There was a rope across the access road to the beach, and a man asked us to give a "dash" to enter the public beach. There was a policewoman sitting there with him, so I reluctantly decided to pay.

The beach is wide and lined with palm trees and many little grass huts. It's dirty, but not filthy. We parked, hopped out and were immediately surrounded by ten twenty-something-year-olds yelling at us to pay them for guarding the car. Who were they guarding it from? There was no one around but them! I said, "We're just having a look at the beach for a few minutes." They started yelling louder now, and not in English, evidently scolding Lawrence for my failure to comply with their demands for money. I yelled back at them "Leave us alone!" The situation was deteriorating. I'd seen men and women fist fighting on the side of the road, and I wondered if they might hit me. Maria looked terrified and just wanted to leave, so we conceded defeat. As we headed back the guys shouted rudely at us and threatened Lawrence. I guess it wasn't our day to visit the beach.

These are a few of the adventures of my first weeks in Nigeria: good, bad, funny, and unforgettable. I'm sure with time, I'll have a better understanding of these experiences. But for the time being, I'm happy to share them with you and have a good laugh at myself and at this fascinating place, Lagos.

Everyday Life

Gems. Photo by Els Van Limberghen
Carrying meat. Photo by Katrina Head
Catching fish. Photo by Ilonka Hoffmanns
Girl and lemons. Photo by Katrina Head

Groundhog Day
By Gail Collins

According to legend, on February second, a furry rodent crawls from his burrow to blink at the day and gauge his shadow to determine the coming of spring or the continuation of winter. A shadow means more snow, and the lack of one means blooms are on their way. If the same groundhog crawled from a sewage ditch in Lagos and managed to dodge the perpetual foot traffic on the side of Lekki Expressway, the sun could surely cast his shadow, but winter's snowflakes wouldn't appear. On the off chance that a stray cloud passing overhead concealed the animal's silhouette, the earth would not be renewed by spring. That reminds me of Bill Murray.

Bill Murray starred in a movie called *Groundhog Day* where an endless cycle of mornings dawned the same day. A replica of the previous 24-hours occurred no matter how he tried to alter the course of events. And he strained through numerous opportunities. Each time Bill laid head to pillow to release the failure of another day, the alarm clock radio woke him at precisely the same time with exactly the same song to confront a day IDENTICAL to the one he'd struggled through only yesterday. That reminds me of life in Lagos.

As the feature star in my own drama, *My Life in Lagos*, I live six degrees north of the equator and as routinely as each day wanes at roughly 6:30 pm, exactly 12 hours later the daylight half begins for me. The sun's shining varies only 14 minutes over the course of a year. In tandem exists an invariable tropicality -

warm and muggy or warmer and muggier. The leaves don't fall into piles that warrant jumping, but consistently drop one a day budding anew a replacement or two. Seasons, months, holidays, even one's own birthday, lack any landmark clues as to their approach. My first year, I forgot Halloween, Thanksgiving and even Christmas until my homeward-bound plane dropped me into the twinkling, tinseled aisles of Wal-Mart.

Upon moving to the Dark Continent, the frenzy to recreate our familiar world within Africa, Nigeria, Lagos and even our company compound powered us. We labored at making a home and a life from a host of random and virtuous details that represented us, our family. Like Bill Murray, we grappled with each day to force the Nigerian culture to accommodate us, but we couldn't seem to change a single thing from getting the furniture we needed to reorganizing the safety elements on a job site, no matter how much energy we threw at the day. And, as life spins out, it is the little things that kill us or drive us to madness or to drink, and that minutiae slowly wore us down. Each time we asked, "When do you think we can get our broken light bulbs replaced /oven door reattached/washer hooked up/new assignment...?" we heard the familiar chant, "Anytime from now..."

Without a schedule of checkmarks to brag of accomplishment, we gave up, or gave in, or relaxed into a near-comatose state. We rose at the same time and bedded at the same time missing birthdays, Mother's Day, winter, spring...

One thing finally saved Bill Murray in *Groundhog Day* from living out a lifetime trapped in the same day - a genuine interest in others. And it saves every expatriate who learns this lesson. Our move to a continent that is strange to us can cause us to act pretty strangely ourselves. Trust and savvy help us to embrace such a foreign place and to come to grips with the fact that it won't adapt to us. When I learned to love Nigeria for its own intrinsic value, I found a new day in each 12-hour sunlit opportunity, and then, *My Life in Lagos* took a shape that I will regret leaving behind.

Pregnancy

By Tony Marley

When I arrive at work each day, the guards normally greet me warmly, "Good morning sir. How was the night?" or, "Welcome, sir. How is the family?" I normally respond by saying that everyone is fine, and asking about their night or family, and pass on by.

One morning, as I prepared to enter the building, the guard said, "Good morning, sir." "Good morning," I replied. "How is your wife sir?" asked the guard. "Pregnant," was my brief reply. He paused for a moment and then responded heartily, "WELL DONE, sir!"

Rain

By Christine Laurenssen

It was rainy season in the African tropics which meant serious downpours unlike anything I was used to in Europe, where it mainly just seemed to "spit." So serious were these rainstorms that after a day and night of continuous rain, the roads flooded to the point that a boat would have been a more useful form of transport than my Toyota Corolla. Unfortunately, Richard, my driver, did not have a boating license, and I did not have a boat. Therefore, we struggled to the office through water so high it reached half way up the car door. The poor Toyota was not quite equipped to deal with this type of weather condition. I was amazed the engine didn't pack up, as all around us cars were breaking down. We developed some serious leakage with the foot-well flooding almost to seat level within seconds. There

Driving in the rain. Photo by Ilonka Hoffmanns

I sat, shoes off and cross-legged in my suit and freshly ironed shirt, on my way to a client meeting. I contemplated buying a pet shark just for fun - it would have been a great way to intimidate street hawkers who were rather starting to get on my nerves with their bizarre offerings of magazine racks, fake Gucci and Rolex watches, rolling pins, hair clippers and other stuff you do not need when you are stuck in a traffic jam - or in this case, a flood.

In any case, poor Richard drove along with water sloshing around his legs and bare feet with his trousers rolled up to his knees. After two-and-a-half hours to reach my destination and four-and-a-half hours to get home, the amusement had worn off and I was longing for the comforts of a road like the M69! I love adventure, but it's not much fun when you're dressed to impress!

A Lawless People

Anonymous

Traffic was hopelessly locked up on Ozumba Mbadiwe, the main avenue along Victoria Island. To avoid the congestion, my driver for the day drove up the wrong side of the road into oncoming traffic catching half the car's wheels up on the median and proceeded to my hotel. When I asked why he was driving in such a crazy way, he said, "We are a lawless people." He got me home; that was his job.

Lagos Driving Manual

By Bob Griffith

Many expatriates acquire driving licenses in Nigeria. Only practical experience can really teach one the rules, but I've devised this pocket Driver's Manual and an exam to aid your comprehension.

MY SPACE: "My space" is where I am now, plus wherever I may want to place myself. OR, more exactly - all of the space between me and where I want to be. This is further delineated by the shortest path through the limited available space in my immediate proximity.

Rules About "My Space":

1.   Always position your car in the most advantageous spot on the road - random placement often works best.

2.   To enforce "my space," drive within millimetres of another vehicle to compel the driver to yield access.

3.   Remind others they may be entering "my space" by horn honking to establish immediate and undeniable rights and provide an impenetrable barrier to anyone considering encroaching from any direction.

4.   Potholes are not "my space," yet "my space" expands as required to avoid one, or two, or three of them.

Important Note: All drivers practice a version of the "my space" law.

DANFO: "Danfos" are Volkswagen-type vans used as buses with four to five rows of seats filled to explosive proportions. The strict automotive safety regulations in Nigeria demand crowding in lieu of seat belts. Air bags can't compare with the tight packing of people and their wares to prevent the launch of even a chicken in the event of an accident.

DANFO SPACE: "Danfo space" is akin to parking privileges on a highway: exclusive spacing.

Rules About "Danfo Space":

1.   "Danfo space" overrides "my space" at any time. The plethora of danfos greatly confines "my space," but these wrinkled, rusted buses inspire self-preservation and obedience to this particular law.

2.   Bus stops can take place whenever and wherever desired. A quick stop in the middle of the road with friendly smiles to all around, and they're off again; no worries, mate.

Important note: Another danfo safety feature is driver visibility. With no suspension and the back loaded with people, the raised angle of the vehicle front naturally affords the driver an improved view of upcoming "danfo space" ripe for the picking. The fare collector is usually the guy who owns the bus and generally stands in the open sliding door and doesn't fall out too often, even after hitting the potholes.

POLICE ESCORT SPACE: "Police escort space" is in the middle of the space race - ahead of cars and behind danfos.

Rules About "Police Escort Space":

1.   Identified by a series of cars and flashing lights, escort teams look impressive, but ultimately, they have nowhere near

the rights of danfos.

2.   One can choose to ignore these escort teams until the lead vehicle pulls alongside and beats the bonnet of one's car with a baton. Their siren, buzzer and retina-searing highbeams create a sympathetic mood. Now, we are taking a leap of faith that there is somewhere for them to go once they are past you, but repeating this sequence does eventually create a path.

NO SPACE (OPTIONAL READING): Some things are best described by what they aren't. The converse to "my space" is naturally, "no space." "No spacers" include: okadas, 10 million pedestrians, bicycles, handcarts, beggars, polo-ponies exercised during rush hour, vendors in go-slows and any other creature unlucky enough to be in close proximity to "my space."

Rules About "No Spacers":

1.   "No spacers" perform a dual function: marking the lanes with their presence and executing an accomplished employment scheme - hawking their goods, ferrying passengers or collecting for charity. A wily government keeps costs under control by not spending their limited funds on things like painting lines in the street and with effective "no space" laws, lane markings become completely unnecessary.

2.   Although "no spacers" are multi-taskers, they do not occupy/claim any premium space. One can ignore them in exercising "my space" rights as easily as a lane change in the Western world.

EXAM:

Enough theory on something as rudimentary as driving by feel and right. Let's go to the practical and true exam.

Driving School. Photo by Bob Griffith

Danfo crowds. Photo by Judy Anderson

Danfo. Photo by Katrina Head

Problem - You are driving from a two-lane side street onto a four-lane road possessing a five-foot median. Make a left turn under the following plausible conditions:

* Traffic approaches from both sides with no stoplight or traffic cop (inconsistent protectors of "my space").

* A danfo approaches from the right and pulls a U-turn into oncoming traffic blocking the flow in at least one "lane."

* Traffic from the left slows giving into exclusive "danfo space," however both directions continue relatively unaffected around the bus utilizing sidewalks as necessary.

* One vehicle proceeds against traffic to find "my space" for himself. He appears to be making a left turn onto the side street where you wait. However, instead of turning into his lane, he pulls away across the side street into your lane.

* There are centimeters of space left over from "his space" waiting to be "my space" and effect your turn. Punch the accelerator, grind a bit of clutch, and...

WRAP-UP: So how'd you do? Did you make it cleanly away? Don't worry; there will be unlimited road tests on every weekend and even on casual trips to the grocery store. Soon, you'll be a road warrior demanding "my space" like everyone else.

* * * * * * * *

Does "my space" really work?

I headed out on a Saturday to research a trip for the Nigerian Field Society. A reconnaissance like this ensures proper planning and prevents poor performance. The first part of the journey was a charm, cruising down a four-car-wide divided highway.

Remember, we talk in "widths" here as no lanes are painted or marked other than by "no spacers," so I use it colloquially. After a very rainy morning, we expected a few temporary hold-ups. The potholed sections of road are the worst and after a downpour, lakes appear. Easing around one of these watering holes, we passed a danfo listing at a 45-degree angle and a vehicle nose-diving and joked that a warning sign on the dirt shoulder should read, "Swim at your own risk."

The homeward journey jammed up 20 kilometers outside of town turning our three-hour outbound trip into an eight-hour return. The rain blockages outbound created huge go-slows, so motorists thought the obvious way around this watery mess was to use the relatively empty inbound lanes. In fact, this was such a good idea that lots of very clever people exercised this option

A bit of a pothole. Photo by Bob Griffith

driving against traffic. There are few breaks in the concrete median, so at some point, those folks on the wrong side of the highway needed to get back on the proper side of the road creating more chaos at the turning point.

A danfo-dominated petrol station stands at this juncture and as danfos are at the top of the pecking order and have no fear of entering oncoming traffic, they chose to cross both the outbound and inbound lanes of traffic for their returns to Lagos. Their migration across the highway completely blocked off the outbound lanes, which were now six-wide versus what was two-wide on our outbound trip. We inbounders, also six-wide on our side of the road by this time, couldn't move forward because of the five-wide lanes of traffic driving AT us the wrong way.

A stalemate? "My space" laws, plus some policemen who were flogging cars with rope whips in an earnest attempt to guard "everyone's space," created a one car-wide lane for us inbounders. Mind you, this happened to exist in the MIDDLE of the lanes of outbound traffic, rather than to the far right side, but after only six short hours in the go-slow, we went merrily on our way. It's a good thing I have a double tank in my car and had brought food.

Postscript: The Nigerian Field Society trip went by boat!

Pest Control

By Gail Collins

"The wheels on the bus go round and round," I thought, "and so do the children." Thank goodness for seatbelts, or I couldn't pin anyone down. It was my last day as Bus Mom. A week full of possibilities had been felled to three return school runs a day. Instead of a life, I had a job - making sure every child got on the bus before being run over in the parking lot; keeping heads from being bashed in by Geography books; and racing after kiddos to deliver lunches or homework left languishing on bus seats to cause calamity later. The children's thoughts, certainly, were on anything other than going to school. On the return end of the day, however, I picked up valuable exchanges on etymology, Indonesia's currency and an origami maneuver that changed ordinary paper into crocodile jaws. Apparently when given the chance, teachers gained enough attention to record data on the blank tapes of a child's mind.

I hadn't been thrilled when the call came to take on this volunteer position. "It's my turn next week," Linda explained, "but I'll be away. Can you please switch weeks with me?"

"Switch! I don't have a week now as far as I know. I'm new. We just got here and school is almost over. Do I have to be Bus Mom this year?" I honestly wanted to hear, "Relax, honey, of course not."

Linda had been tactful instead. "Couldn't you please take it on? If you don't do it now, you'll be stuck with the last week of school..." She made that option sound sinister.

Apparently there was no ducking this duty. It was merely a matter of sooner or later since my children rode the private company bus from our compound to school a few blocks away.

In the days leading up to "B Week," stray remarks galvanized my initial reaction - this wasn't a coveted position nor for the coward. Few ladies liked being Bus Mom. Lips twitched and warnings flew. Sharon called it Pest Control. That helped me feel less the cad for dreading the job since they ranked the post directly below oven cleaning.

When Monday came, I swayed and hugged my coffee mug in the parking lot at 6:45 am sharp in the damp, humid morning. "I'm sick" had been my first waking thought in the cocoon of my bed. Now, I was sure of it. My second thought had been "Can I write an excuse?" like the ones I penned for my children to stay home and be indulged. Instead, I'd put both feet on the floor, a thermometric hand to my forehead to confirm fever and got dressed like a grown-up.

While waiting to board the little 18-seater bus, I hauled a boy off of an eight-foot stone wall he thought would assist his experiment with flight. Manhandling children generally contradicts my nature. Even after birthing four opportunities of my own, I'm more of a mind to see how a situation plays out - observe and apply crisis management, with ice as necessary - but pavement and gravity are undeniable constants. And hooking kids by the belt loops is just too easy. As the day took shape, I shook a bit here and there, but didn't throw up on anyone. I was sure that would've set off the vomitable chain reaction I'd once witnessed on a bus ride in Junior High School. Despite my ills battling the children's spiraling volume of piping voices,

I catalogued a few names that day. Like Superman's - Eric.

Tuesday, my nausea and fever fled leaving only a remnant headache complemented by a cough punctuating what could have been a conversation had an adult happened by. As for the children, I pegged and book-ended the deafening ones while separating the child most prone to convulsions resembling punches to the arm of unwary neighbors. Amidst this, the week quickened. By Wednesday, I knew every child's voice, habits, snack preference and name. This came in handy for barking Robbie's attention when he leapt seat over seat bunny-style, and when Sam's game of "slap happy" threatened tears. Through such neighborly engagements, I distinguished their squeals of delight from those of pain. On Thursday morning, I realized I secretly pined for the children, curious as to what mischief they might attempt. That afternoon, I shared a sack of cookies with the busload of revelers. I loved this pleasant distraction in my adult day. As I let their AM energy boost mine, on Friday, I heard a little girl's voice over the din.

"You look pretty today, Bus Mom." It was Natalie. I smiled. Her comment made me feel pretty. Natalie's lip jutted out as she added, "It's a shame today is your last day." I sighed and agreed. I winked at Natalie and instantly, her gap-toothed smile returned mine. Even on the short rides of life, friends can be made along the way.

An Okada Can Be Your "Life Vest"

By Orietta Skarstein

It was my first day as "Bus Mom." I had to pick up the younger children from their classrooms at 1:30 pm and escort them to the bus. I was very anxious and nervous, especially about being late or leaving one of the smaller kids behind. So, my driver and I left home at 1:15 for the 5 minute drive to school.

Suddenly, I realized it was already 1:20 and we were still next to our compound! I explained to my driver why we needed to get to school immediately, but his only answer was "Sorry Madame, we will get there, but we are in a go-slow!" My impatience was growing by the second!

By 1:25, we had not moved. To my increasingly anxious remarks, my driver now answered "Sorry Madame, we will get there, but we are in a go-slow!" I started to picture the little Pre-Kindergarten boy crying when he realised that he was the only child in his class who hadn't been picked up. Ten seconds later, I pictured all the moms of the compound rioting against me due to my irresponsible behavior of not picking up their kids on time. Oh my goodness!

It was time to take action. I told my driver I was going to walk to school. He answered that it was too dangerous for his Madame to walk in this awful traffic jam. I was surprised he was so protective of me, acting as my body-guard. Finally, I think he understood my urgency and told me it was better to ride an okada… "A what?"

He stopped a motorcycle taxi and asked the driver to take his madame to the school. "Drive her safely... Don't run too much... I'm watching you... BASTARD!" I didn't know how to hold on to the bike or the okada driver, what to do with my purse, where to put my feet... and in that precise moment I tried valiantly to recall the Pre-K boy crying!

We had ridden one block, when I realized several people were laughing and shouting at us. The okada driver turned around and told me to put my feet down because it could be dangerous as we passed by the cars.

Two minutes later I started to feel a nice breeze as we picked up speed and finally made progress. We approached the school security checkpoint and I told the okada guy not to stop. I just waved my school identification and all the drivers around began to laugh and shout, "Look at that madame!"

Orietta's okada experience. Photo by Jo Demmer

We bounced to a stop outside the school and it was time to pay. My driver had told me to pay between 30-40 naira, but that day I was out of small bills and, of course, out of time to ask him for change. He thanked me profusely as I handed him a 200 naira note.

Everything went perfectly. I got to school at 1:29, just in time to pick up the Pre-K boy. Oblivious to my great adventure, he greeted me politely, the punctual Bus Mom.

The next day, I met two friends who told me they had seen me driving on an okada with a great big smile on my face!

Count Your Blessings

By Jodi Adeyinka

Living in Lagos has taught me to appreciate many things that I normally take for granted. I never realized how fortunate I was until I came here. I no longer leave water running while brushing my teeth and I wouldn't dream of leaving the lights on when exiting a room. When I pick up the telephone and hear a dial tone, I'm happy. If I go to the store and can find everything on my list, I'm thrilled. If I can make it from point A to point B without encountering a "go-slow," I rejoice. And at the end of the day, as I lie in my cozy bed in my air conditioned room with my husband by my side and my son down the hall, I thank God for my many blessings.

To Stop or Not to Stop

By Kerri Hakala

To stop or not to stop: that is the question: I think I have the answer.

On the way home from a late night, I was confronted with a police checkpoint in Lekki and asked to pull over to have my "papers perused." I would have thought that any sane person would show whatever papers were necessary to peacefully arrive home to the loving arms of their spouse. This was not the choice of my driver. He tried to run the roadblock and brought a little horror into the lives of the ladies entrusted to his care. After being forced at gunpoint to stop, we were all subjected to the anger of the police. In the light of day, perhaps they were justified in their anger. They are surely confronted daily with unsavory types who have a desire and a reason to flee justice. Three ladies coming home from a night of Bunco do not qualify. I have never been so afraid for my life or felt so responsible for others. While the police were yelling and punching my driver through the window, we tried to phone for help and to calm the ruffled feathers of the police. Help eventually arrived in the persona of company-provided Kevlar-covered security guards. The standoff finally concluded when my driver stepped out of the vehicle as originally requested, which appeared to pacify the policemen. The situation came down to POWER... just who has it was made painfully clear and was a frightening lesson for all of us. This can be a dangerous place and the choice to stop or not to stop will be easier the next time around.

Thinking and Driving

By Moyo Adeleye

One morning, I drove down Sanusi Fafunwa Street on my way to work. I leaned my chin on the knuckles of my closed left hand, resting my elbow on the door as the cars crawled along.

All of a sudden, a policeman jumped in front of my car, waving frantically for me to pull over, which I did. I wondered what I could have done to cause a problem. As I rolled my window down, he began yelling at me, accusing me of using a cell phone while driving, which is illegal in Nigeria. Maybe my bent hand looked like a phone, fair enough, but as I opened my palm, he recognized my hand was empty. In disbelief, the officer accused me of dropping my phone the moment I spied him. "I'd have to be a magician to make my phone disappear that fast," I said. I dug in my purse and retrieved my phone to put the policeman in his place. He insisted I check my list of calls for him. I calmly handed my phone to him. Caught off guard, the man explained that he pulled me over because I was a hazard to other road users.

Finally, the officer leaned over and said gruffly to me, "I'm being lenient with you, but next time, you're going to the station for thinking and driving." Thinking and driving, an offense? Only in Nigeria.

Hope

By Julia Yeoh

Nigeria... the name of the land into which we, from another realm, are thrust - lock, stock and barrel. As such, we expat spouses share this common link. I remember sullen, silent thoughts when this desultory name arose from the dark pits of Africa. Nigeria, the Neverland of woes and throes. Nigeria, "Never ever land," imbued fear at the outset but now it has become a nicety. We are by necessity, nicely ensconced after some initial conundrums and quibbling doubts.

I scan through the papers for ideas on what to write. Baffling thoughts. Bemused, I look at the faces of the natives - Yoruba, Igbo, Hausa. I look at their myriad faces uttering, "Mirror, mirror on the wall, Is there any fairness at all?" I cringe at the austerity around me, heightened by a general sense of desperation.

We are searching for an identity, a lonely quest for answers. Many have come, many have seen, many have conquered their fears and phobias - claustrophobia, xenophobia to name but two!

By now, after at least three or four months of acclimatization, we arrive at a certain consensus in our journey. The initial restlessness has given way to a sense of purposefulness. Our kids are settled in school, the be-all and end-all of their existence here. We miss the comforts of home and familiarity of loved ones, but by gradual disassociation through time and distance, we grow somewhat detached from these attachments and accoutrements. We are plunged into different cultural mores but we will survive... with God's grace. Happiness is indeed our aim, to quote Aristotle, "The meaning and purpose of life, the whole aim of human existence."

We cling to our pragmatism. Make the most of what we have here, a road indeed less travelled. See the stars in the skies. See not the mud and shambles, look beyond the ephemeral to a better tomorrow.

We now reach the next stage in our voyage of discovery. We are becoming accustomed to hardship and dereliction, but not necessarily dehumanized. From Cable TV, our lifeline, this aphorism smiles at us: "Connect through culture, Celebrate diversity." Expatriate wives, I see beauty in your faces, your movement, and your serenity. I come away with a comfortable sense of belonging although sometimes feelings of negativism nudge at me.

Everywhere I go, I witness a dark sea of people surging, rushing. Urgency is written largely in a "now, now" syndrome of living. Some struggle from hand to mouth. They are happy, yet hapless people; their kids still laugh and play. Yes, I see deprivation in their dusky faces, and feel the nuances of poverty settle on them like flies.

I listen to them as I ride on their bumpy roads. On dog days, a certain sense of panic and deja-vu fill me, along with dire expectations, and ennui. I will journey through the "here and now" again and again, before finally acceding to my fate in this land, not of a million sorrows, but miracles. For whilst there is life, there is Hope.

I end with a quote by Nathaniel Hawthorne, "Happiness is a butterfly, which when pursued, is always just beyond your grasp, but which, if you will sit down quietly, may alight upon you."

The Big Boss

By Jo Demmer

One day, I told our company-assigned driver that I needed him at 1:15 pm. He asked if he could bring the "big boss." I inquired why the big boss wanted to see me, and he said he needed to take some drivers to a conference and they would see me too. Mystified, I realised that I wasn't going to be enlightened by pursuing the conversation further, so I said, "That's fine."

At 1:15, I went outside and saw my driver standing proudly in front of the staff bus, along with eight other drivers! As the penny dropped that he meant the "big bus," I cracked up laughing.

A Nigerian proverb says
"A man who eases himself in public,
gives cause to others to despise him."
Photo by Bob Griffith

The Pantry Sale

By Jodi Adeyinka

Garage sales and yard sales are common, but pantry sales are a unique practice among departing expatriates who shipped in too much food from their home country. Some people have walk-in closets for their clothing, others have walk-in closets for their food! A pantry sale usually takes place in someone's kitchen, dining room, and/or pantry.

You often see the same faces at pantry sales - we're the ones without the luxury of an annual shipment from home. Sometimes I feel like a vulture, circling overhead until I hear that someone's leaving, then swooping down to snag chocolate chips.

Not all pantry sales are alike. Some people will try to sell you items that have expired, while others will jack up the price! My absolute, all-time favorite pantry sale was held by my dear friend Johara. It was by invitation only, so I was grateful even to make the exclusive guest list. Johara was extremely organized - she gave each of us an itemized list with the price she paid and the selling price. Prior to the sale, we walked around three huge rooms piled with mountains of food, even one full of cleaning supplies. Once the sale started, we were all civilized; no pushing or shoving, we simply piled things up in our own corner of the house. I spent several hours and several hundred dollars. One year later, I still haven't finished everything and nothing has expired. The only thing I don't like about pantry sales is that it means the person holding the sale is moving away. But that's another story...

The Butter Man

By Clare Brown

Like many expats in Lagos, I am keen to save money on my exorbitant grocery bill, so when possible, I buy in bulk. Basil sells butter in 10 kg boxes wrapped in 250 g packs, a reputable brand. I order a box or two and split it up between my friends. Basil is reliable; he comes more or less when you expect him and has never let me down... until that day.

I'd ordered 10 kg, but Basil said his new supplier would only do 20 kg, so I said, "OK." He turned up at night, just as I'd got the kids to bed and was ready for some peace and quiet. I didn't check the butter because I was tired. After a little relaxation, I opened the box and was horrified to see a 20 kg yellow butter block staring back at me. It was too big to fit in my freezer, the thought of splitting it up was scary.

I fumed for not checking the butter when it was delivered and blamed myself for being tricked. I phoned him up and was outraged when he acted as if it was the normal packaging. More angry now at being taken for a fool, I asked him what he was going to do to rectify the situation. He agreed to sort it out the next day. I thought, "A likely story."

Much to my surprise, the next day, Basil picked up the butter without complaining about the open box and returned my money. A few days later, he arranged a box of wrapped blocks of butter. My faith in Basil, and humanity, was restored.

Phone Etiquette

By Kerri Hakala

Answering the telephone properly is something, I daresay, most mothers try to impress upon their children. Let's face it, no one wants his or her beloved offspring to grab the line and say, "What do you want?" Having lived in America, Asia and currently Nigeria, I have realized that phone etiquette is subject to cultural nuances. In Asia, I was amused to overhear many cell phone conversations where the call recipient merely said, "'ello… Ah… Ah… AHH… Ah… OK, BYE!" I wondered what could possibly be communicated in such a one-sided manner. A typical "American" phone conversation involves a greeting and then efficiently getting to the point. Not so in Nigeria. I was completely baffled and annoyed as I was adjusting to the new etiquette.

"Ring Ring"

Me: Hello.

Caller: Good Day, Madam.

Me: Yes?

Caller: How are you this glorious morning?

Me: Uh, fine… How may I help you?

Caller: And how are the children?

Me:… Just fine! Thank you… How may…

Caller: Praise be to God!

Me: Uh… Yes… Uh, who is calling?

Caller: And how is your mother?

Me: Fine! Who is this?

Caller: This is John, main gate security.

Me: Yes???!!!…
Caller: David, the Artist, is here and would like to come up.
Me: I do not need to see him.
Caller: Do you want him to come up?
Me: NO!!! I do not need to see him.
Caller: When can he come?
Me: Not today, I have plans. (I am going out, have to wash my hair, am doing a bikini wax… whatever can be thought of at the moment!)
Caller: So… you do not want me to send him up?
Me: NO!!!!!
Caller: All right, Good-day Madam.
Me: Good Day!
Caller: And tell the children good day…
Me: Thank you…

Finally, hanging up with a sigh, I went about my business. Five minutes later, the telephone rang. It was my friend, Linda, who lives in our compound.
"Ring Ring"
Me: Hello
Linda: Hi! This is Linda. David the artist is coming to my apartment… want to come by?

The realization that I need to slow down when answering the telephone has helped keep my blood pressure stable. The truth is that spending a few moments to be polite and hear someone bless God is not such a bad way to go about your business. I think most of us could benefit from a little praise and blessing in our lives. This is one of the many lessons I will carry with me from my stay in Nigeria. So don't be in too much of a hurry when you call me… Good Day!

Roads

By Christine Laurenssen

Breaking news! The massive crater in the Lekki access road, caused by the floods seven months ago, is finally being filled in! It is believed that a large number of okada drivers, unsuspecting motorists, horses and small goats were recovered from the hole before they began.

Also, men with a freaky death wish are drawing white lines on the Third Mainland Bridge, actually dividing the freeway into 3 separate lanes! I do wonder why they insist on (a) doing it by hand and (b) attempting to complete the project on hands and knees during morning rush-hour. So far, two cups of coffee have been spilt over my good trousers as Sunday, my driver, braked to perform crazy swerving maneuvers at the very last moment to avoid these kamikaze line-painters who suddenly pop up in the middle of the freeway.

Pothole News Brief - Lagos Desk

By Gail Collins

On May 11th, a Mixed Softball Tournament was held at the AISL campus to include many of the expatriate companies in Lagos. The team jerseys all looked so much alike that even before one beer, the players could not tell themselves apart. The tournament was held strictly for weekend warrior fun. In fact, this rule was stressed in the comical guidelines, emphasized by the final point - should there be any discrepancy as to the final standings, the winning team will be determined by the downing of a beer for speed. Unfortunately, this unprecedented ruling never came to bear. Pat O'Brien, who oddly enough owns Pat's Bar and Grill, a popular expat hangout, supplied free food and drink.

During the afternoon, as is typical during the rainy season, a huge thunderstorm blew in. Tragedy struck. Awnings set up to provide shade for fans had not been staked properly, or at all, as it came to light, and were responsible for the chaos that erupted. Our on-the-spot reporter witnessed the events firsthand. A gust of wind threatened to lift one of the coverings off the ground as support poles fell aside. Several men standing nearby grabbed at the roof supports and side canvas to hold it down. The crowd then watched in horror as two men floated up fifteen feet in the air when the tent acted as a parasail. One rider, Ken Tillman, held on and alighted deftly onto a narrow concrete wall, akin to Mary Poppins, while the cover continued to rise and crash over the nine-foot barrier. The other man was not so lucky. He let go, dropping hard to the ground below.

The fall guy was identified as Larry Kapler. Immediately, nurse, Anna Kate Owens assessed his injuries. Jim Collins happened to be standing next to Mr. Kapler and used his own baseball jersey (yuck) to tie up Mr. Kapler's wound, then bare-chested, accompanied the man in the ambulance to the hospital.

As is common in cases of trauma, Mr. Kapler was medevac'd the next morning to Johannesburg, South Africa. He spent the next two months in traction for a fractured pelvis and damaged hip joint in addition to a broken elbow. It should be noted, ironically, that Mr. Kapler is the Lagos Health and Safety Manager for an oil company, and the third consecutive one to sustain a serious injury. Hmmmmm. The track record does not look good for lost time injuries, but the team effort is alive and well.

People to Meet

Gems. Photo by Jo Demmer
School girl at Ishahayi Beach. Photo by Ben Wilkins
Lady carrying baby. Photo by Katrina Head
Nigerian dancer. Photo by Ilonka Hoffmans

A Wise Old Man Once Said

Photographs by Tiffani Wetherbee

Traditional Nigerian Proverbs

Old man, Kano Market

A child's face
is his

Little boy, Agaja

mirror.

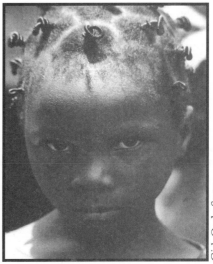

Girl, Ondo State

One must row
in whichever boat one finds oneself.

Mineral seller, Benin

Okada, Epe

Family, Lekki

A single tree
cannot make a forest.

Drinking boy, Obraka

Anyone who urinates in a stream should be warned because any of his relatives may drink from the water.

Greatness
and beauty
do not belong
to the gods
alone.

Little girl, Agaja

Floating boys, Abraka

I t is a pot of water that is already half full
that the World would like to help
in filling to the brim.

Girl, Lekki

Girl, Tarkwa Bay

Girl, Tarkwa Bay

An old

Chief of Bar Beach, VI

Old man, Abuja

banana leaf

was once

young and

green

Smoking man, Ebute-metta

Rastafarian boy, Bar Beach

The gods may still send
a gentle breeze
when they want to bless us.

We are what our thinking makes us.

Old man, Abuja

He who
is called
a man
must
behave
like a man

Tuareg man, Kano

Hausaman, Bar Beach

An oil lamp feels proud
to give light
even though it wears itself away.

Gourd maker, Kano

Saving Grace

By Gail Collins

Patience didn't show up for work. She'd left mysteriously the afternoon before. Now it was Tuesday, and during lunch, Bob's cell phone rang. "Patience," he mouthed to me - Bob's secretary and a Nigerian national. By his compassionate tone and the fissure drawn between Bob's brows, the evidence Patience presented cleared her AWOL status. But her story revealed that someone else was seriously missing. Patience hoped to see her sister alive.

The day before, while at work, Patience received a call on her mobile phone. The caller said her sister was dead, but gave no details of why, or who he was. Patience was struck by the irrationality of it. She hadn't even known her older sister was in Nigeria, as Grace now lived in South Africa running an export business. Was the call even true? It was too horrible to ignore, so she went to the police.

The officer in charge, Sunday Ugbe, fiddled with his badge, which flashed under the fluorescent bulb of his office. The man didn't get up nor offer Patience a chair. "Yes, we received the same call. We suspect she is dead. Still, a kidnapping is possible."

"What?" Usually unflappable, Patience vibrated. Coiled like Medusa's snakes, thousands of tiny braids framed her smooth face where a single vein danced on her forehead. "Which is it? Is my sister alive or not?"

"I do not know," Ugbe stood and yelled back at her. "If I saw her body, I would know she is dead. Now go. It is my job."

"I cannot just go..." Her tone pleaded now as she smoothed her manicured hands across her skirt, and alternately, tugged at the hem of her navy blazer. She waited. She craved more information.

"Hmmm?" Sergeant Ugbe looked at Patience, then through her and yawned. He shrugged his shoulders and sat back down to dial the phone. In one fluid motion, he kicked back in his seat and dismissed her with a wave of his hand as he chatted amiably into the phone, but not to someone who had any intentions of helping Patience.

Turning hard on her heel, Patience bolted through the filmy glass doors of the police station, tears spilling and searing on hot cheeks. Why would the police think Grace had been kidnapped? Had money been mentioned? And who in this city of 20 million people could have spirited Grace away? Why would no one help her? Her head filled with questions, yet the police were content to wait for some sign, or perhaps a body, to surface and mutely answer them. Her shoulders shook three or four times as a cry broke from her tight lips. Then like lightning, everything seized, something molten inside her forging steel under the sweltering sun. Her fists balled, she marched to her car. By the time Patience made that call to Bob, she was angry, not desperate anymore. She needed two days she said, "to think and to act."

Connections are important in any country and especially in Nigeria. An air of calm now surrounded Patience, the detective, as she began working angles on her case. She wondered about tracing the incoming phone number, but sure it was from one of a thousand rickety roadside stands that sell mobile phone calls by-the-minute. Many people simply didn't have phone service. Either the man wouldn't want his call traced back to his own residence or he had no phone. She prayed he was stupid and wireless. And that she could find him.

The next morning, a determined Patience showed up at the police station again. "Can you order a list of calls made around the time when that bad man called about Grace from the phone number that showed up on my phone yesterday morning? If there is a number called frequently, we could trace that number to the address of whoever owns that telephone. Talk to the owner about people who phone him regularly." Sergeant Ugbe glanced across to his underling parked in the chair nearby with lids half-closed, and they shook their heads. "We would have to get such things approved," Ugbe said and stretched. They didn't look like they were about to interrupt a lifelong coffee break to get that done.

Later that day, something did turn up. "Miss Grace's purse, but not her body," Ugbe said over the phone sounding more annoyed than relieved because the wrong thing had showed up. "That's good news," Patience said to reassure herself, yet she feared time was more critical than ever. Favors were called in - a friend working at Nextel phone company ran the list of calls from the original phone number for her. Sure enough, a number she assured herself was called by the maniac holding her sister showed up five times from that phone. Was it someone the killer called routinely or was she way off in the jungle beating the bushes for snakes?

Patience took the number and no explanation of its origin to the police betting that it was called from a roadside stand that Grace's villain used regularly. If she could locate the address of the roadside stand, maybe the owner could identify the caller who would lead them to Grace. True to apathetic form, no one at the police station asked the question of Patience, "Where'd you get that number?" But they did trace the address for the original number. On the spot. A roadside mobile phone, just as Patience thought.

Responding like a kick to the groin from information falling into their laps, the police doubled over in their efforts. All at once energized, they sped in the police car to the dirt site address on Ajose Adeogun Street of Mr. Olorun's GSM phone stand. Horrified by this visit from the police, Mr. Olorun forgot to greet the important policemen, jabbering on in an attempt to disassociate himself from whatever harm now appeared to include him.

Sergeant Ugbe wrapped his long fingers around Mr. Olorun's upper arm, and the blathering stopped. In smooth tones, Ugbe said, "Please, we're here as friends. And friends give help to each other. We have just a few questions for you. But first, how is your family, Mr. Olorun?" And with passion, Ugbe proceeded from there.

Mr. Olurun recognized the phone number listed five times and remembered the threatening caller. "I don't usually listen to people on my phone," he said, "but his eyes were mean." Mr. Olorun thought the number the man called belonged to a friend. "Maybe his friend. I don't know him," Mr. Olorun stressed. The Sergeant called the number from the stand, then drove to the home of the caller's friend. And with a reaction and cooperation paralleling the phone stand owner, this fellow led them to Grace's abductor.

After arriving at the police station, Ugbe announced brightly to the accused man, as if he were in line for the grand prize, "All we need is a confession and Miss Grace Akingbade's location.

So..."

The accused's lanky body remained slumped in a broken wood chair, his face impassive, and he said nothing. So, Ugbe's lackey pulled out a big stick, cranked it back like a bat and fractured the man's leg with it. Instinctively, the man reached forward. A yelp and a curse escaped his lips before slowly and stiffly, he leaned back. Eyes squeezed tight, a tear tracked a shiny trail before splashing on the concrete floor. As beads of sweat bloomed on the man's forehead, he quietly admitted to making the calls to Patience and the police about abducting Grace Akingbade.

"I don't know if we can believe him," said Ugbe finding his momentum as interrogator and winked at his partner. With purpose and a smile, the sidekick shattered the man's other leg. At this, the condemned clutched the chair, and between rasped breaths, divulged Grace's whereabouts satisfying the police with the consistency of his story.

By Friday evening, Grace lay recovering in the hospital from the trauma of being blindfolded and drugged for three days, while Patience finished a day of routine secretarial work. The motive for Grace's torment remained unclear, but Patience suspected a crazed lover, someone their family refused to support Grace marrying - a shrewd assessment on their part of someone who'd be hard-pressed to stand on his own two feet at this point. Ah, sex and intrigue. These elements transcend every culture, but how many sisters perform the investigative work, calling in favors just shy of breaking a couple of legs to unravel their personal horror?

A final thought, if I were ever in trouble, I'd want to be Patience's friend.

A Prince of a Proposal

By Marilyn Thomas-Penney

I recently accompanied friends to an afternoon business/social luncheon at the country home of a local Nigerian prince. At 10 am, the prince himself drove his Land Cruiser into the compound to pick up our group. I smelled trouble when he then could not maneuver his vehicle back out of the garage. Too fast and furious, with one hand on the wheel and his head wrapped around his guests' conversations, the prince gave us a white-knuckled ride out of town. With stomachs heaving, we arrived at the prince's old, dilapidated colonial house.

Soon after our arrival, the power went out because his generator had exhausted the supply of diesel fuel. We sat in the sweltering heat trying to converse. The prince did then what any host worth his salt does to save a party cooking in its own juices; he broke open the liquor cabinet. The finest champagne naturally led to red wine chased by beer, and with time, we upgraded to brandy. Our social mores oiled, the conversation supernaturally turned to the importance of sexual potency for the Nigerian male. Perhaps, the prince assumed that fatherly fertilizing is a uniquely African necessity for procreating.

As this adolescent atmosphere continued, the prince looked at me and said, "You would make a perfect wife. You are educated, you stand up to me, and oh, you are sexy. And since you have your own job and money, you are inexpensive." Such criteria are certainly flattering. But then, he proceeded to tell me what he would like to "do" to me if I came back to visit. I was taken aback by the whole proposal so candidly endorsed by descriptions of how nice life in the future could be. I laughed it off. A friend's business relationship was at stake, and after all, it's not every day that a 59-year old professional woman gets such a prince of a proposal.

Signed,

Not Actively Looking (for such a prince)

The Invisible Man
By Jodi Adeyinka

A Nigerian was about to travel out of his homeland for the first time. He had heard about trouble faced by Nigerians traveling abroad, so he went to his village to consult a witch doctor asking for protection from any problems he might encounter. He was given instructions and warned that they would only work outside Nigeria.

When the man disembarked from the plane in the US, a uniformed official approached him and said, "Sir, please come with me." The man confidently walked over to a wall, stood beside it, and then lifted one of his legs, as instructed by the witch doctor. The official said, "Sir, put your leg down and come with me." The man was perplexed. He slowly turned towards the official and said, "You mean you can still see me?" to which the official replied, "Yes." Shaking his head in disbelief, the man walked away with the official. Apparently, the man was told by the witch doctor that by standing next to a wall and lifting his leg, he would disappear!

When Help Is No Help At All
By Christine Laurenssen

Household help is seen to be one of the benefits of living in Nigeria. I found some terrific staff in my year in Lagos, but only after surviving a few disasters. Here are some extracts from my journal about three of my staff headaches. Read on.

The Maid

I have long suspected that Ann, my maid, has been taking advantage of my continuous absence from the flat while I am at work by using the phone and eating my food. It now emerges that she actually had a little enterprise going on and let the drivers from other households use my phone. You can just imagine the scene; "50 naira for a phone call to anywhere in the world for as long as you want! Come on people, it's a bargain, get it while you can, Madam will be home soon!"

As Ann is employed by my company, I left the delivery of the good news to Wilomena. Head of administration, she is nice but rather scary looking at six-feet tall, six-feet wide and moustached. As Ann would probably have made off with half of my belongings, Wilo smartly took away Ann's keys before breaking the news that unfortunately her employment had ceased.

The Driver

In the mean time, good old Dozie the driver, who I was really beginning to like, did something so eternally stupid I have unfortunately had to relieve him of his services as well.

One Friday night, Akin, Vinnie and I with a group of my colleagues, headed to the mainland to see a live music show called Lagbaja - a saxophone player and his band who play every last Friday of the month at Motherland in Ikeja. We gathered at the venue by twelvish and indulged in some Nigerian Star lager. In the meantime, Dozie was having his own little party drinking cheap local brew for 30 naira a bottle.

By the time we returned to the car at 4 am he was asleep in the drivers' seat. Akin knocked on the window a couple of times. Dozie did not seem to hear a thing. After literally banging on the door with both fists Dozie woke in a confused and dazed state, and tried to open the door without unlocking it. "Unlock the door," Akin shouted through the window. Dozie continued to fumble with the electric window slide, failing miserably to do anything except arouse more frustrated banging on the window from Akin. Finally, our drunken driver decided it was all far too much effort and lay back down in the seat and closed his eyes.

Abruptly, all talking stopped. We gathered around the car and peered through the window in utter amazement at a comatose Dozie. At once, everyone started screaming for him to "Open the #!$@#! door straight away or else!" This seemed to have some impact, as Dozie finally managed to get out of the car.

While a disorientated and confused Dozie stood by the car and mumbled senselessly to himself, I stuck my head through the passenger door and had a good sniff. Hmmm, strange, no alcohol-smell whatsoever! I looked at him, wondering what type of drug he had consumed. As Akin and Vinnie debated who was going to drive home, others joined our crowd: a beggar with one leg and another with two useless limbs who maneuvered around on an adapted skateboard thingy focused at crotch height. People kept tripping over him. The volume of conversation grew louder and louder, as more random people joined in, assuming it was their citizen's duty to advise Akin on what he should do. Chaos ensued.

Suddenly, Dozie piped up that he was fine and insisted he could drive home, no problems! Without further ado, he jumped back in the car, closed the door, started the engine and revved it nonsensically, his seat still in the lying position. Just as Akin grabbed the door handle, Dozie released the handbrake, still revving wildly and launched the car across the road and straight into the concrete road-divider. And that was how poor Dozie signed his resignation letter...

The Cook

I have now experienced the epitome of staff headaches. After we sacked Emile, our docile and slightly stupid-looking cook for untimely-ness, stealing and other general annoyances, he showed his mean, calculating side. We suffered two weeks of his non-stop phone harassment and impromptu "begging-and-pleading-to-get-his-job-back" scenes at the office. One afternoon, as I stepped out of an important client meeting, only to trip over Emile crouched in front of the conference room door, anger took hold of me. I told him in no uncertain terms, "Piss off and leave me alone or I will press harassment charges against you!" Now I don't know if a charge like this actually exists in Nigeria, but he seemed suitably impressed and left.

According to Emile, he had not been paid for all the days he had worked during the last month. In fact, Emile worked only seven days during November and had been paid accordingly. He said he had been cheated out of three-quarters of his salary; because when a worker disappears for nine days on the trot he should be paid for the time he spent gallivanting around town drinking cheap gin and sleeping with his neighbour's wife. Right?

My outburst obviously got him thinking. Not long after, whilst friends and I were enjoying a Saturday night at Pat's bar on Victoria Island, I received a call from our upstairs neighbour, Jan. Two armed policemen were at the flat claiming they were coming to arrest me!

Emile, who according to his last sorry diatribe had not a penny to his name, had managed to bribe the two men into coming to the flat together with their AK47s. There, they engaged in some general shouting and intimidation of the compound security guards before attempting to move on to their eventual target: me. But I wasn't there. It was a big disappointment for them to be greeted by Jan, who is probably one of the best-connected South Africans in Lagos. He wasn't intimidated by all the noise. Instead, he invited them into his flat, told them to sit down and shut up and without further ado called their sergeant in charge, Jan's personal friend. They dropped the intimidation act within a nano-second as they realized that big wahala was coming their way.

They required that I come down to the police station for a chat. Unfortunately, I was too busy drinking Becks to engage in such activities and Rule Number One in Africa: never go to the police station! So a company representative was sent the following Monday to sort out the whole mess and after some customary shouting and bribery, the matter was laid to rest.

Imagine my surprise when shortly after this fiasco, I received a phone call from none other than Emile!

"Madam", he said "Madam, hello, it is me, Emile!"

"Yes, hello Emile, what do you want?"

"Please Madam, I want to talk. I do not want to talk about the past; I now want to look to the future. Please can we meet to talk?"

"Talk about what Emile? As far as I'm concerned there is nothing to talk about."

"Madam, please, we need to talk abut the future. About you and me and the future... and my job."

"Goodbye Emile..."

Ice from the Sky

Anonymous

On one of my routine business junkets to Lagos, the houseboy at the apartments asked, "Where you come from, does ice fall out of the sky?"

I laughed and replied, "Yes, it sure does, we call it hail or snow."

The Trailing Spouse

By Jo Demmer

What do these women have in common: a teacher helping motherless babies, a psychologist playing Bridge and an engineer working out in a gym?

Of course, they are all highly intelligent, well-educated and attractive, but there is something more. They are all married to intelligent, well-educated and attractive men (a bit of flattery never goes astray, I find) whose jobs have taken them to remote parts of the world. This has meant that, by choice or by circumstance, these women have ceased paid employment. They have assumed the role of the "Trailing Spouse," as did I.

As a one-time professional woman in command of my own destiny, earning the title Trailing Spouse has involved a huge mind-shift. The term itself conveys less than flattering imagery. "Trailing" has connotations of being pulled behind, of relinquishing free-will; like a cavewoman being dragged by the hair at the caveman's whim. The word "spouse" implies that this person is not the main attraction, merely the other half. Haunted by images of women sitting around playing Canasta and drinking gin and tonic all day, I had a palpable fear of becoming a mindless card-playing junkie. I realised that I needed to define myself by something other than my job.

One year into my new role, I feel somewhat more qualified to describe this phenomenon from now on referred to as TS. Careful observation has indicated that there is much, much more to being a successful TS than knowing how to shuffle cards. This research revealed that the genus TS breaks down into species with unique characteristics. Armed with this new understanding, I have developed a scientific mode of classification for the stereotypical spouse. It is called the BAG (Beautiful Articulate Girl) system and is described as follows:

The sports BAG: The super-fit, always running, always swimming or always tennis-playing woman. She flaunts a perfectly toned body and makes you feel guilty for eating chocolate and lounging by the pool instead of swimming laps. She is further identified by her choice of the quintessential sports gear - Nike and Reebok are the order of the day. There are many sub-species of the sports bag such as the **golf BAG, tennis BAG, gym BAG,** etc.

The shopping BAG: She is regularly spotted at Lekki and Balagun markets or the latest fashionable art gallery, never tiring of bargaining and shopping, shopping, shopping... Beware her credit card when the shopping BAG visits Dubai, New York or London and especially her hometown.

The school BAG: With at least two or three children at school, she is devoted to helping the school. She holds positions on the School Board or the PTA (Parent Teacher Association) or both and spends more time at school than her children do.

The evening BAG: You know the one, the femme fatale of whom every woman is jealous and to whom every man is attracted. The one oozing cleavage and self-confidence. She is present at every social function (at least every evening one) and is always impeccably dressed, coiffed and made up. Also referred to as the **corporate hand BAG**, she is the perfect accessory to help her husband get ahead at work.

The duffel BAG: Always travelling back home or to other exotic destinations around the world, she earns more frequent flyer miles than there are okadas in Lagos.

The cooler BAG: She is the cool, take-it-easy spouse. Unflappable, chilled-out and relaxed. Not to be mistaken for the **wine BAG** who is also chilled-out and relaxed, but needs the fruit of the vine to induce this state of mild euphoria.

The charity BAG: An example to all of us, she tirelessly champions for those less-fortunate - motherless babies, starving masses, school-deprived villagers.

The work BAG: A rare breed, this woman works full-time on location. Usually, she is employed at the same company as her husband, although some are teachers or nurses. In extremely rare cases, she may even be the trailer, not the trailee. This raises questions about how to define the male variety of the genus TS: a **mail BAG**? Or, with any luck, a **money BAG**.

The tea BAG: She rushes around being busy, busy, busy. But, no matter how busy she is, she always finds the time for a cuppa. Could also be the **coffee BAG**. Look out if the tea or coffee BAG is deprived of caffeine for too long, she might just bite your head off!

Yes indeed, the TS is a rich and varied genus. Their lives provide opportunities for fun and games - after all, what's wrong with a G&T or three? But many of these women also use their time to learn from and give back to the community, be it to their host country, their children's school or their fellow expatriates. Money is raised for worthwhile causes, motherless babies are cuddled, schools are built, and cross-cultural understanding is improved.

Having begun my time as a TS with a certain amount of suspicion and fear, I am now proud to be amongst their ranks.

When sizing up a newcomer in our midst, I mentally take out my BAGs from the closet and try them on her to find the closest fit. Will she sit on her patio drinking a chilled bottle of wine from designer glasses? Will she jog around the compound in her midriff top and sexy shorts? Or will she be the next champion for world peace? I ask myself: "What kind of BAG is she?"

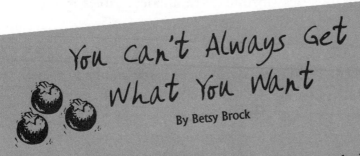

You Can't Always Get What You Want

By Betsy Brock

Betsy lives near the top of a high-rise apartment building and her balcony gets plenty of sunshine. Since she and Randy love fresh produce, Betsy planted some tomatoes. As the plants began running, it was time to stake them. Banking on the ingenuity of drivers to find just about anything, she told hers she needed some small sticks. "Maybe some bamboo, like the scaffolding around here." Less than an hour later, her driver stood smiling at the door... with eight-foot bamboo poles. Betsy had him bring the poles out on the patio, grabbed one and plunged it into a pot. "Whaddya think?" she asked him. "I think your plants can grow very high," he suggested. And as the Rolling Stones sang, "If you try sometimes, you just might find you get what you need."

Male Seeking Mail

By Ben Wilkins

I've never considered myself an anomaly; eccentric and a bit unconventional maybe, but not one of a kind. This was brought into question at a recent evening with a trailing spouse and her husband. I realised that our positions were juxtaposed and that I was, indeed, a trailing spouse myself, dubbed a mail BAG[1]. Having spent seven months blissfully unaware of my social standing in Lagos, I had no idea that I even needed a classification. Coming as something of a bolt out of the blue, it was unnerving to be tagged BAGGAGE[2] and warranted further investigation.

The dinner date rumour mill brought to my attention that the trailing spouses of Lagos were given column inches in this book to explain their kind. In the interest of sexual equality, I requested permission to rant in the same manner as BAGs frequently do.

So, after a brief, and it must be said, superficial contemplation on the subject of trailing spouses as it relates to gender, I would like to try to de-mystify the mail BAG. The male trailing spouse is certainly less complicated than his femail counterpart. But, then again, isn't this always the case? He is, however, far less common, rarely understood and often treated with suspicion.

---

1. Defined by The Trailing Spouse, by Jo Demmer

2. Either an encumbrance or a Buff Accomodating Guy Going Around Grabbing Empathy

To begin with, the male version of the Beautiful Articulate Girl prefers to be known as the Buff[3] Accommodating Guy. This rather extraordinary fellow is unknown to the majority of the population, as he only exists in the darkest shadows of society; I myself am proof of this. As the only mail BAG specimen in Lagos who has crawled into the light, it's not possible to offer a complete classification of the genus, but I can offer a little insight through my own experience. I would suggest that the BAG bloke is likely to be adventurous and outgoing; without a need to prove himself - or he would not agree to tag along behind a girl. Bumping along for the ride is an opportunity for travel, without having to worry about where the next pay-cheque is coming from, rather than a slur on his employability, or manhood.

In my own circumstance, after resigning myself to the idea of following my partner to Africa, I ensured it would be as much fun as possible. Instead of flying to Lagos, I bought an old Land Rover and drove it down from London. Trailing my partner by a month or so, I fought sand in the Sahara, mud in Mali, and finally, the labyrinth of Lagos.

Initially, I had hopes of spending countless days mounting expeditions into the Saharan Interior and sending monthly requests for a top-up on the gin and tonic supply - for the anti-malarial effect of the quinine you understand - and enough fresh meat and charcoal to keep the BBQ fully stocked. Unfortunately, the BAGGAGE handler didn't see things the same way. Being the bill payer, she vetoed my plan.

3. Used to describe the male that is handsome, chiselled and muscular

So, I had to stay put. But settling into Lagos, as the sole representative of an entire genus, proved frustrating. The females have clubs and parties to entertain them and pass the time. Typical MALEs (Men Active in Lagos Employment) do guy's stuff like poker nights, but how does the mail BAG get in touch with them? Contact with the suit and tie brigade of the expat world can be tricky outside the office.

In an attempt to better integrate the mail BAG into Lagos society, I propose the inauguration of the MAIL BAG (Mulling Around In Lagos Begging Appreciation Group). For starters, there'll be a weekly "Wednesday beer morning" at Pat's Bar. I may be a solitary figure propping up the bar, but you're welcome to join me because sympathy is appreciated and encouraged.

Tina

By Ilonka Hoffmanns

When Tina met her boyfriend, she could have never guessed what the future would bring. She thought only that he was nice, a good-looking boy. The two had met in the market where Tina bought vegetables. She had tried to manage the bags herself that day, and then suddenly, he had appeared next to her. "My sister! Where are you from?" he asked, and Tina looked up to see a beautiful face and his handsome clothes. With a giggle she replied, "I am from Ondo, so are you!" as she heard in his dialect that he came from the same state as she.

They talked for a while, and then separated. Tina's mind fluttered. What happened just then? She felt a tingling feeling inside her. He was so handsome, so well dressed, so friendly! The tingling in her stomach spread to her whole body, and she sensed a deep warmth. She was in love. She quickly looked over her shoulder to search for the boy, but he was gone, and she realised she was disappointed. That night, Tina dreamt of him.

The next day, Tina went to the market again, hoping she would see him. She stayed there for as long as she could, but he was nowhere. Her shoulders bent over in despair on her walk home. Then as suddenly as before, "Sister, how are you today?" She looked up. It was him! She wondered, had he followed her? She tried to hide her happiness, not wanting him to see how much she longed for him. Again they talked. When she came home this time, she held his phone number. Tina memorised the numbers on the paper in her hand.

Soon, Tina and the boy started a relationship. She adored his attentions and only hesitated for a short while when he pushed her to have sex. "I love you so much," he said. In her heart she wondered, was it not a bit too fast? Was it wise? But when his arms curled around her waist, her thoughts went only to that one exciting idea, and Tina fell into bed with him. This became normal between them, and their relationship started to look as if it had been there forever.

Except one thing had changed - Tina noticed his interest in other woman. Had he done that before? Had she been so blind with love that she hadn't noticed his roving eye for beautiful women? Was he having sex with them too? Just the thought of it made her sick. About that time, she started waking up nauseated with her ill thoughts. "It's just a reaction to my boyfriend's escapades," she thought, but despite her excuses, her period didn't come. The shock of it made her body tremble. Was she pregnant? Oh no! She didn't want to marry that boy; she didn't trust him. Her love for him was breaking apart. What could she do?

Tina couldn't sleep, and days went by before she confronted him with the news. The boy looked at her in disgust. Suddenly that lovely light in his eyes disappeared. Now Tina saw him for whom he really was. "You must undergo an abortion," he said, looking at her slightly swollen tummy. "I do not want to have a baby." He made it clear: a baby would not fit into his lifestyle, and she had no other option. Worse, Tina knew she would loose her job if she kept the baby. She thought of her mother and wished she could talk to her. Her mother would've understood, but her parents had died a long time ago. Tina was so very alone.

The boyfriend turned his back to her physically and suddenly, there was no money for her either. He didn't even want to help pay for the abortion, so Tina went to a local doctor on her own. The procedure was painful. Why did it hurt so much? She screamed with agony, yet the nurses said, "Be quiet." Was this her punishment? She yielded. Then, it was done. The doctor gave her a bag of pills and told her to rest for a couple of days.

Tina went home, crawled into bed and dreamt of the baby in her tummy crying out for help. She woke up terrified and noticed her bed soaked with blood. For a moment, she thought her dream might be real, but then realised she had lost a great deal of blood from the abortion. Struggling to get up, Tina groaned, "Oh, this hurts so much!" She fainted.

When Tina woke again, she lay in a growing pool of blood. Slowly she rose. Her legs were weak, so she held onto the chair. Such a mess! Tina moved herself to the basin, got some water and started to clean the floor. Hearing the noise, Femi, her friend and neighbour, came to check on Tina and walked in on the pathetic sight. Seeing all the blood, Femi urged Tina to go to a doctor, but she refused, "My money is gone. I am already in debt and have to manage on my own."

Femi cleaned the floor and her bed, then, helped bathe Tina. She cooked and put Tina to bed, but she couldn't leave Tina, so Femi slept on the floor beside her bed. The next morning, Tina felt exhausted and couldn't stay awake. Femi helped her out of bed and put Tina in a chair. The rest of the day, Tina thought only about the baby removed from her tummy, this image imprinted on her mind. She cried herself to sleep that night, and again woke with terrifying dreams and bathed in blood. This time it was less, but no less horrible.

The days went by. Every day Tina felt stronger, and the shocking experience became part of the past. Tina's present was the pain and the wound. The blood slowly turned into a smelly, yellowish discharge. It poured out of her all day dirtying her clothes and didn't stop. As the days turned into weeks, the aching and the messy flow stayed. People started to ignore Tina or move out of her way, pulling up their noses from the strong odour.

Weeks became weary months and the months, a lonely year. Tina, the beautiful girl turned into a smelly, grey woman whom no one came near. Only her closest friends still talked to her. But amongst all this, something good happened; Tina found another job working for an expatriate family. As soon as they heard the story of Tina's ordeal, they helped her, paying for surgery in South Africa. The surgeon was surprised after examining her. Tina's womb had been torn by the abortion and pieces of infected foetus still clung inside. It caused both the soreness and the rank discharge.

The doctor cleaned Tina's womb and took tissue from another part of her body to repair the punctured womb. When Tina awoke, she felt the change within her. There was discomfort from the surgery, but it was different, not as agonizing. The doctor warned her, "Stay away from men for the next two years. You can't take the risk of getting pregnant. If that happens, your womb will rupture again. It must grow strong."

With pain medication, Tina healed quickly, and soon was able to walk around. Within a week, she recovered enough to travel home to Nigeria. The first thing she did was to visit Femi. As Femi opened the door, her mouth fell open. What a change! She saw a different girl, the one she remembered from before she met the boyfriend. Tina had bright eyes with a sparkle in them. She looked wonderful again, smelt like a soft flower and wore clean clothes. There she stood - a healthy, happy young woman. Through tears, they hugged. And despite Tina's loss, a new life had begun.

Plant Wash

By Mary Walker

Mary was dashing out the door for a meeting when she brushed by a potted plant, noticing the dull, dusty leaves. "Blessing?" she called to her stewardess. "See all the dirt on the plant's leaves? Please wash all the plants in the house so they're shiny green again." When Mary returned that afternoon, she gasped at the sight of multiple clothes lines strung through her kitchen filled with beautiful clean leaves each carefully pinned in place to dry.

The Lowdown On Food In Nigeria

By Stephen Head, age 14

I wanted to find out more about our cook, Eddie Agyarko. He is the first cook we have ever had, so I asked him a few questions. He is busy in our kitchen every day and cooks better than my mom! Eddie loves to work with flour. He bakes brownies, cakes, lemon bars, muffins, cinnamon rolls and pita bread. He can even make our favorite Tex-Mex recipes with his homemade tortillas.

Eddie says his favorite cook is Mr. Lawrence, who was his boss for six years. Then, Eddie came to work with expatriate families. First, he worked for a family with two kids, then for a teacher and her family. Eddie came to our family a year and a half ago. Since all his jobs have been for Americans, he is very good at American dishes. Our favorites are poppy seed chicken (our recipe), hamburgers, chicken tetrezzini, lasagna, enchiladas and more. He loves to experiment. In fact, Eddie wanted a subscription to Cooking Light magazine for Christmas. He also likes sharing his talents with other cooks in the compound and he has taught several cooks how to prepare tortillas.

Eddie learned his great cooking techniques from working in a restaurant, and this led to his love of cooking. He wants to own his own restaurant someday and have people working for him. Eddie is so fun to be around and such a great cook, it would be great to take him back to the States with us, but I guess I should give my mom another chance with her cooking skills.

Nigerian Soup

By Jo Demmer and Gail Collins

Vegetarians, be warned: this recipe contains concepts sure to offend. This soup is prepared for special occasions, such as a funeral. When I told my driver, Sampson, I was going home for the funeral of my 95-year-old grandmother, he was most excited. "In Nigeria," he said, "this would be a HUGE celebration! They would kill at least five or six cows." I believe the number of dead cows is proportional to the magnitude of the occasion, and Sampson insisted they would party all night. The following soup might be difficult to follow in a Western kitchen, but give it a go in the backyard!

Step 1: Kill as many cows as the occasion entails (let's assume this has already taken place).

Step 2: Douse the still intact cows with kerosene.

Step 3: Set the cows alight, so all the skin and hair burn away. Stand back so your skin and hair don't. Perhaps ask a neighbor to borrow a flamethrower, to light the cow from a distance.

Step 4: Let the incinerated animals cool, no wire rack necessary, before peeling off the charred bits from the blackened cows.

Step 5: Borrow a machete from the flamethrower friend and cut the cows into large chunks.

Step 6: Fry the cow chunks in a humongous fry pan over an open fire. Maybe the machete man possesses such a skillet.

Step 7: Place the browned cow chunks in a party pot or a 30 gallon drum with water, tomatoes, onions, pepper and seasoning.

Simmer the concoction over an open fire for several hours.

Step 8: Invite everyone you've ever known, especially the flamethrower-machete-giant-fry-pan owner, over for your celebration feast. Serve with pounded yams or rice.

Enjoy!

Cooking at New Market. Photo by Katrina Head

Pounding yams. Photo by Bob Griffith

Graduating from Pre-K

By Jo Demmer

The children in my son Tom's graduating class of Pre-Kindergartners (four year olds) were greatly excited. Several of the mums, including me, spent time at school making graduation caps out of black cardboard and red ribbon. Moving up was a BIG deal! The ceremony was a fun, but serious affair at which the children sang songs and recited a poem:

"We live in Nigeria where the sun is hot.

We live in Nigeria where it rains a lot.

We live in Nigeria where we swim and play.

We live in Nigeria hooray, hooray, hooray!"

Though the song and poem involved cheering and enthusiasm, none of this showed on Tom's straight face. His complete lack of expression made me giggle. The children came from Nigeria, Malaysia, South Africa, America, France, Denmark, Israel and Australia. The school principal handed certificates to the children whilst solemnly shaking their hands, saying, "Way to go!" Each child then proceeded to the professional photographer who finally got them to smile.

Jacob's Education

By Jo Demmer

Once upon a time, in a very crowded city in Nigeria, there lived a little boy called Jacob. Jacob, who was six years old, shared his two-room home with his parents and his younger brother, Samuel. Although his family did not have much money, Jacob knew that he was a very lucky boy; he went to school and when he grew up, he intended to be a doctor. Many other boys of Jacob's age would never be blessed with a formal education.

Jacob's mother, Faith, had never attended school, but she had a steady job selling food on the side of the road. Every day, Faith would take up her position marked out by a couple of wooden boxes; hot and dusty in the dry season, hot and muddy in the wet season. A fire burned steadily under the large pot of boiling oil into which she would drop spoonfuls of batter, fishing them out when they were golden brown and selling these "beans cakes" for 10 naira each. Her generous smile displayed white teeth as she greeted each of her customers cheerfully, "Ekaaro," to which they enthusiastically replied "Ekaaro."

Jacob's father, Wednesday, who had not attended school either, had a good job driving for a rich expatriate family. His boss, whom he addressed with the traditional term of respect, "Master," did not like to drive in Nigeria where the push and shove tactics on the road were foreign to him. It was easier and safer for him to have a driver who understood how to survive on the roads. He endeavoured to be a kind Master, and he knew that without an education, the future for Nigerian children looked bleak. So as well as a monthly salary, he gave Wednesday money to pay for his children's schooling. For his part, Wednesday drove safely and treated his Master with great regard.

Jacob loved school and he studied hard, listening to everything his teachers told him. Soon he learned to read and write. Popular and intelligent, he was nearly perfectly happy. But Jacob had a problem. Although the other children at the school were not wealthy, they always appeared to have more money or things than he did. Sometimes a pencil, sometimes a notepad, sometimes a special treat for lunch. Always something.

One day, Jacob sat in the corner of the playground and refused to play with the other children who laughed and sang and jumped about. David, his best friend, came over and asked, "Why don't you play with us?" Jacob explained, "You and Stella and Lucky and Thomas are all getting 200 naira to go to Mr Biggs next week. I asked my mother and she said I can't go. She said, 'No my boy, that is an extravagance we cannot afford.'" He mimicked his mother's voice so well that David started to laugh.

Jacob frowned, "Stop your laughing! It's not funny! To make matters worse, Mrs Obe just said we have to buy a schoolbook for 300 naira. Well, I know my mother will give me money for the book, but there is no way she will change her mind about Mr Biggs."

David smiled and looked around to make sure that nobody else could hear him. Then he lowered his voice and confided, "My mother won't give money for Mr Biggs either. So I will tell her that the book is 500 naira. That way, she will give me enough money for both. So you see, my friend, your troubles are over."

Satisfied that he had solved his friend's problem, David joined the other children in their play. Jacob sat and pondered on this cunning plan. His heart felt sad about the plan, but his head thought that it was very clever.

After school, Jacob asked his mother for 500 naira for a school book. Faith sighed, for to give Jacob 500 naira, she would have to sell 50 extra beans cakes. Then her spirits lifted as she thought of Wednesday's Master. She told Jacob that she would ask his father.

That night, Jacob curled up in the bed he shared with his brother and pretended to be asleep, but all the while, he thought and listened. He heard his mother ask his father for 700 naira for the book. After hesitating, Wednesday replied that he would ask his Master for the money. His voice sounded a little strained. Jacob's face did not move, but inside his head, he smiled, for he had learned an important lesson. His heart still felt a bit sad.

The next day, Wednesday asked Master for 1000 naira for a school book for Jacob. Master was a little surprised being asked for more money when he was already paying for school fees, but he wanted to be fair. So he took out his wallet and gave Wednesday the money.

On the way home from work late that afternoon, Wednesday bought a fresh, juicy pineapple for 300 naira. That night, Jacob, Samuel, Faith and Wednesday enjoyed the fruit and Wednesday proudly handed Faith 700 naira for Jacob's school book.

Before school, Faith gave Jacob 500 naira for his school book and then went out and bought a special loaf of bread for 200 naira. This bread was her family's favourite, and she knew that they would feast on it with pleasure. Jacob trotted happily to school and bought his book.

The next week, Jacob enjoyed a real treat of some fried rice with his friends at Mr Biggs. It pleased Jacob's head that his plan had worked so well and as time went by, he used a similar plan to buy things like popcorn or simple treasures. Once he bought a special pen with four different colours - red, blue, black and green; simply press the coloured buttons to choose which one. Over time, his heart forgot that the plan had made him sad.

Some months later, Wednesday approached his Master for more money for Jacob's school. Master was not pleased. He said "Wednesday, I have been very generous with you, but this is too much. Stop asking me for money! I have given you enough!" Master was getting suspicious that the money he had given for school books was more than the school books were worth. He made a note in his mind to check with a friend how much money they gave to their driver for school books.

Wednesday did not enjoy being rebuffed by Master. He felt cross with Faith and cross with Master. Because he was so irritated with Faith, that night he yelled at her, "Woman, you have got me into trouble! Stop asking me for more money all the time!" He upset her so much that she cried and cried. Because he was so annoyed with Master, the next day when he went to buy drinks for him, Wednesday did not give back all the change.

Master had a very bad day at work. His project, already over budget, suffered further delays, and his contractors demanded more money. Customs had increased import duties or "facilitation payments" so supplies that Master needed were going to cost more and take longer to arrive. Master felt cheated and frustrated. This reminded him to check with his friend about school books. His friend's answer made it clear that Wednesday had tricked him. Master could not understand why Wednesday had not been honest when he had treated him so well. That night when he saw that his driver had not given him the right change for the drinks, his frustration turned to anger.

When Wednesday arrived at work the next day, Master accused him of stealing. Knowing that he had been found out, Wednesday thought quickly and concocted a long tale to explain the missing money. "I bought the drinks and came back to the house to leave the change. When I was counting out the change my wife called on my mobile phone. She was very distressed and said that Jacob was sick and I should rush home right away. I left that minute. On the way home, I realised that I still had some of your money in my pocket."

Master listened quietly, but his anger grew as he saw the skill and apparent ease with which his driver could lie. Wednesday tried to cover his increasing sense of panic by furrowing his brow into what he hoped was a look of sincerity. He put his hand in the pocket of his trousers to produce the 500 naira, but it was not there. Trying to maintain his outer calm, he assured Master, "I wore a different pair of trousers yesterday. The money must be in the pocket of those trousers. I will bring it to work tomorrow."

Master no longer trusted Wednesday. He did not like having things stolen, and he hated being lied to. Master fired Wednesday. Despite Wednesday's begging and pleading, Master remained firm. Wednesday returned home, devastated.

* * * * * * * *

Now that Jacob's Daddy did not have a job or a master to pay for school fees, he could no longer afford to send Jacob or Samuel to school. They finished at the end of term. Without a letter of reference, more months went by, and Wednesday was still unable to find another driving job. He could no longer pay for anything much at all. Faith worked harder; she stayed later at work cooking more beans cakes.

Jacob was upset that he had to stop his education. He knew he needed to learn much more to become a doctor when he grew up. Wednesday promised that as soon as he secured another job, Jacob and Samuel could go back to school. In the meantime, the two brothers went to work at a market carrying purchases for rich people who came there to shop. This way, they earned enough money to buy some food for their family.

One day Wednesday's former Master came to the market with his wife. As they drove into the car park, a swarm of children surrounded them, vying for attention and begging to be the lucky one chosen to be their boy. They chose Jacob, although they did not know who he was, as they had never met him. They jostled through the market with vendors clamouring for them to inspect their wares of woodcarvings, brass statues and other local crafts. Jacob trotted along behind, carrying their purchases - a batik tablecloth, a game of Ayo, a strand of glass beads to drape around an urn and several necklaces. When they returned to their car, they gave him 100 naira for his efforts. Jacob admired their brand new Toyota Land Cruiser and thought that if ever he became a doctor, he would drive a car just like it.

As their new driver drove them home, Master and Madame discussed the issue of children working at such an early age instead of going to school. Seated in the comfort of their air-conditioned four-wheel drive vehicle, they agreed on the value of education in breaking the cycle of poverty.

Places to go

Gems. Photo by Jo Demmer
Cows at Eleko Beach. Photo by Gail Collins
Eleko Beach. Photo by Judy Anderson
Abeokuta. Photo by Ilonka Hoffmanns

Masquerade

By Michelle Ukoh

I reeled in horror as the cruel whip lashed around my body. Fear, pain and reluctant admiration coursed through me as I cowered beneath the towering giant costumed in blazing array. His menacing mask glowered at me, and I gripped my camera tightly. My tormentor yelled at me in disgust, gathered his whip and stalked away to rejoin the parade. Too stunned to speak, my brain flashed through the events that brought me to this moment.

My love affair with Nigeria began 23 years ago when I was posted in Lagos as a young American intern for a telecommunications union. I gained an appreciation for African art, people, music, culture and life. I loved the energy and spirit of the country. I returned to the USA and my fate allowed me to meet a man who embodied these things, and I married this wonderful Nigerian. His family embraced me and have been the world's best in-laws. For years we lived in the USA.

We now live in Nigeria with our two children. Our favourite place is our ancestral village Ndiamazu, Ikpakwa, Arondizuogu after which we named our son Amazu. Each April, we travel there to participate in the celebration of the yam harvest festival (Ikeji) which lasts for three or four days. Most Igbos feel disconnected if they do not return to their village during this special time. Some travel every year from all corners of the world: China, Russia, USA, Britain and more. On the eve of the festival, yams of the previous year are disposed and on

Day One, new yams are offered to the ancestors. Yam fufu (like mashed potato), okra (a long green pod) and pepper soup are the chief foods for the festival, and family and friends visit each other's homes feasting throughout the day and night. My husband and son eagerly anticipate Ikeji believing it brings them into communion with the departed fathers of the clan. It is a great occasion for giving thanks and honouring our ancestors.

The highlight of Ikeji is the Masquerade event. Igbo men decorate themselves by painting exotic patterns on their bodies and dressing in traditional clothes - billowing, multicolored fabric strung with bells and baubles - crowned by ferocious masks bejewelled with beads and cowry shells. Some walk on stilts, beat drums or throw flames as they parade from village to village to perform dancing and fighting rituals. Competitions are held to show respect and strength to appease the spirits. Some Igbo people believe the Masquerades are involved in black magic (juju). Hundreds of years ago when the Masquerade began, women were not allowed to watch the parade; if a woman was caught, she was automatically flogged with a cane, branch or whip. In modern times, however, women are permitted to watch the glorious Masquerades as they pass by their village.

Five years ago on a sunny April day during an Ikeji celebration, I got caught up in the excitement of the brilliant costumes, jangling bells, hazy smoke, screeching children, festooned cars and fevered drumming. I was thrilled to see some of the dangerous Masquerades nicknamed "High Tension," "Corpse" and "The Prime Minister of Masquerade, Pericoma." I took out my 35mm camera to take a picture to show my relatives in the States. So when the tallest masquerade stopped before me, I delighted thinking he stood posing for the camera. My joy turned to horror as he wrapped his lengthy, leather whip around my entire body. As it squeezed the air from my lungs, I saw stars! Around us, the street festival continued; the noise, breathtaking decorations and crazed revelry creating sensory overload.

I didn't scream or cry. I froze, completely shocked. It is forbidden to take photos of the Masquerade, but I hadn't been told and my husband wasn't there to protect me. Even as I broke tradition, I gained respect for the mystique and splendor of the occasion. I promised myself to treasure the photo privately. My female relatives and friends admired how stoic I was and started chanting, "Nwa nyi, nwa nyi!" (Our wife, our wife!) Nonye, my daughter, smiled at me, and Amazu proudly said, "I'm glad my Dad married a strong woman!"

Canned Response
By Kathy Eckert

Three friends and I were walking through a market one day trying to keep our heads low, but white is white against a sea of black skin even in a place as colorful as Balagun. "Oyibo! Oyibo!" the sellers shouted to catch our attention. We giggled to ourselves thinking of the translation of oyibo: "peeled one," meaning all our black skin has peeled away to reveal the white flesh beneath. As more vendors took up the call, "Oyibo," we simply tuned out the noise until one lady yelled, "Hey you, who eat things from cans." We burst out laughing and gave her a smile. We'd never been identified by that feature before.

Lekki Market

By Dakshina Kaushish, age 9

Lekki Market, Lagos is your typical Nigerian market, with the usual buying, selling and bargaining going on. It is extremely busy, with sounds, smells and sights all around you. Some people will offer to carry your purchases for you for a fee, so if you're doing a lot of shopping, it's best to hire one of them. The sellers there offer all kinds of things, and here is where your negotiating skills come in handy - excuse me, did I say negotiating? I meant bargaining. Okay, bargaining isn't as easy as it looks, and some people haven't even needed to do it before!

One of the unique aspects of Nigerian markets is their art. Their crafts are truly exquisite and can be found nowhere else in the world. An ordinary person may scoff at these crafts, but they are treasures in the eyes of many. Some eye-catching pieces are six-foot giraffes, masks, bronze statues, baskets, string-art pictures and lots of jewellery.

All in all, Lekki Market is an interesting and lively place. A child like me could easily get lost, with its endless rows of shops and sellers beckoning you!

Lekki Market. Photo by Katrina Head

Lekki Market. Photo by Katrina Head

A Ram and a Goat Do a Little Dance

By Sophie Wells

My husband, Mark, warned me, "We're Guests of Honor at the Harvest Festival for the Catholic church where our driver belongs. They're raising money." I say "warned" because, although mass is a truly beautiful experience, the auctions afterward go on and on.

Mark and I were told that people donate items to be auctioned off to raise money for the church, and with our driver's help, we decided to offer a goat and a ram. Our driver, Daniel, was thrilled and went straight out to buy them the next morning. As Mark and I sat around the breakfast table sipping coffee, I said in all seriousness, "You don't think he'll put those animals in our car, do you?" We have a small sports utility type, but still... Mark said, "Of course not. The folks Daniel buys them from will deliver them to the church."

Later, at that same table eating lunch, our driver walked in with a big smile to ask if we'd like to see the goat and ram. Nervous, I said, "Are they in the car?" to which he replied, "Yes." Mark's mouth popped off, "You're sh*!ing me, right?" Daniel's face fell, and he quickly said, "No?"

Outside stood two smiling Nigerian men, the goat owners. Ceremoniously, Daniel opened the back of our car. There on plastic sat a huuuuuge ram and a goat, legs tied and sliding around in their own poop as it smeared everywhere. I mean everywhere. At that, Mark looked at me and grinned, "I'll go get the camera." We paid the owners an extra 1000 naira for the land on which the animals stood ingesting their meals till then, and that night, our flock grazed at our driver's house. Some goats, some poop and some money - I thought our big adventure/ commitment was complete.

The ram and the goat. Photo by Sophie Wells

The next day Mark said, "Oh yeah, I forgot to tell you, we have to bring our offering to the front of church during mass." What! Yes that's right, and in full Nigerian regalia - a long overshirt with slits up the sides and pants underneath for the man while the woman wears an ankle-length dress with a huge head tie that resembles an enormous bird nesting in her hair. So, that's how we looked at mass. Our children were totally mortified. Our family is part of an animal offering parade, but we don't march forward. In fact, our instruction is to dance our goats down the aisle "the Nigerian way." This means lean forward a little and make your top half sway while your bottom half juts out and sways the opposite way. Of course, all of this is done while walking and dragging our animals and our children. Whoever said white men can't dance; well, they should have seen us.

As we stood at the back of the church, I said to the kids, "Unless you want to embarrass Daniel, you'd better dance. And smile!" Four boys waited to pull our goat and ram to the front. I say "pull" because our animals weren't any more excited about this trip down the aisle than the kids. While holding steady for the cue to dance, our goat proceeded to fertilize the church entry, and before we knew it, the palm leaves surrounding the archway began to rattle and fall as our hungry offerings munched on what were meant to be decorations. This should have been enough, except a rooster (another offering) broke loose flapping his wings in a mad way causing all of us to race around.

Finally, it was time for us to enter the main hall. Flanked by 15 Nigerians and the four boys dragging the ram and goat, our family made the trek down the aisle. Festive music played and a variety of drums beat out a happy rhythm. We wished everyone could have seen us sway, wiggle, shake and jiggle our way to the front. Even the kids. I'll never forget the day, especially as we were told, "How can you dance like that? You are white, not Nigerian."

Half and Half

By Katrina Head

Kids! I have five, and they're seeing it all through our travels. After living in Lagos for eight months, our family finally flew home to Houston. During our London connection, we waited in the queue for coffee, and my five-year-old son, James, tapped me on the leg to ask, "Mom, why is that lady a Texan on top and a Nigerian on the bottom?" I looked and after a second or two, giggled, realizing a pale British Airways stewardess had on black stockings!

Sitting In Church

By Marla Kunfermann

Powerful air conditioning! This is possibly the number one factor I prized as a white woman looking for an African church.

The first time I visited this cool church I was the only oyibo. It was Easter, and 90% of the women wore African robes and wrappers. And those marathon head ties; they run on forever. The woman slouching on the wall beside me wore a sapphire and gold head tie that matched her shoes and handbag. At one point her monstrous head tie bumped against my Ascot-styled hat as we jockeyed for space for our headgear. I told her, "I think our hats are trying to do battle." She said sweetly, "Mine will win." I believed so, for if might is more, she certainly had more fabric invested in her head tie than I had in my entire dress.

Happiness Udoh and Rose Essien in head ties. Photo by Jo Demmer

The service was FABULOUS - the traditional Easter story with all the trimmings. And of course, the music could make a deaf man cry. The singing matched the beauty of the church, which was spectacular, especially the three huge, wooden, exterior doors, carved from top to bottom.

A couple of amusing things made the day memorable. The minister begged us to be strong and resist the temptation of joining juju cults. It's obviously a real war of culture and faith. More interestingly, he reminded women not to succumb to the lesser, but binding, cults of gossiping and spending. Which just goes to show that while the problems of man can be cultural - trying to keep four wives happy - the problems of women are possibly the same the world over.

The best thing about the service was my two-year-old pew mate with his terribly young mother. This boy was absolutely fascinated with the hair on my arms. Since Africans are pretty body-hairless, I'm sure this was a phenomenon for the little guy. He would sidle over till he and I were practically in full body contact, and then slowly put his hand out, five fingers splayed, then rub along my arm. He especially liked to brush the hair the "wrong way" or touch one hair at a time.

When the minister announced it was time to dance, I decided it was time to leave. This white woman cannot sing or dance. My departure couldn't have gone unnoticed as those carved doors were two storeys tall, and opening them meant casting a sunbeam bright enough to flood a movie set. My friend and his mother made a point to say, "Goodbye and please, come back." As always everybody was friendly, cheerful and welcoming. That's Nigeria!

Funtopia

A revealing story by Jo Demmer

I am not the greatest daredevil; furthermore, I am scared of heights. So, what possessed me to go down the water slides at Funtopia? This fun park contains a huge array of amusements: jumping castles, table tennis, crazy golf, a toddler play area, a game arcade, a climbing wall and pools with water slides. So why the slides? They sound like innocent fun, but this insane apparatus is definitely not for the faint-hearted. Maybe it was peer pressure: my friend, Leslie, also agreed to go.

To reach the top of the slides, we climbed a scaffold-like structure with stairs. Each step had two misaligned wooden slats, so naturally, I stubbed my toe. The stairs were not enclosed - looking down induced awful vertigo. The 12 metre structure housed two slides; one from two-thirds the way up and the other, a near vertical drop from the top.

The first slide did not look too intimidating, just a gentle, varied slope. The attendant gave us our instructions, "Lie down. Cross your arms across your chest and hold your shoulders. Cross your legs." They seemed unnecessary precautions for an innocent-looking slide. "Are you ready Madame? I will push you."

"Aghhhhhhh!" Gathering incredible speed, at a point I became airborne. Splash! I completely submerged in the pool at the bottom. When my legs had stopped shaking, I managed to turn to face Leslie at the top of the death-trap and give her the thumbs up. She too emerged from the pool a few seconds later, laughing and spluttering.

It was now or never for the big slide. With an impending sense of doom, the stair climb was worse the second time. By the time we reached the top, the gentle breeze at ground level felt like a gale. Perched atop a tiny platform that felt on the brink of collapse, with hurricane-force winds threatening to whisk us away, Leslie went first. Stranded on the precipice, I listened to her screams of terror as she went down a sheer drop that looked about 100 metres. My turn was next.

Forcing the attendant to promise for the tenth time that it was perfectly safe, I lay down in the launch position. A gentle push, and I felt myself freefalling until my inevitable crash landing. It was in this manner that I experienced a practical demonstration of the primary law of physics: every action has an equal and opposite reaction. My descent resulted in the equivalent ascent of my bathers. For the uninitiated, let me explain the colloquial term "wedgie." Derived from the verb "to wedge" meaning "to cleave or split," wedgie describes the rather unfortunate situation where the underpants or other apparel enclosing one's backside wedges between one's buttocks. This unpleasant situation can result in sensations ranging from mild discomfort to excruciating agony. A prank played by some juveniles is to give a wedgie to their friend by wrenching the friend's pants upwards from behind. But I digress...

My bather bottoms produced a wedgie of magnificent proportions, and my top flew wildly askew. Now I understood why there were so many pool attendants waiting at the bottom of the slides. I'm not sure how much I revealed, or whether it was just a near miss incident, but it was certainly not the most dignified position for any self-respecting madame to be in. I grabbed desperately at my bikini and hoped that the huge splash

I created upon re-entry had camouflaged my slip-up.

As I passed the pool attendants to find my towel, I was uncertain whether their hearty smiles and congratulations were due to my brave display or my unwitting peep show. I strode over to my children expecting to be given a hero's welcome. "Wasn't Mummy brave?" I cajoled, beaming with the glow of a survivor. "No Mummy you were a scaredy cat - you screamed!" Replied my 5-year-old earnestly. Well, some people are never satisfied!

Mixed Drinks

By Judy Anderson

My father was a U.S. Marine in World War II, so I was excited to attend the annual Marine Ball in Lagos. It was a wonderful evening, full of pomp and circumstance, ceremony and uniforms, good food and drink. Toward the end of the evening, as we had consumed enough wine, my husband asked the Nigerian bartender for "A coke and a diet coke." Our jaws dropped as the bartender carefully poured half a glass of coke, then directly on top of it, half a glass of diet coke. I guess we got exactly what we asked for!

Police Checkpoint

By Tony Marley

One Sunday morning, my wife, daughter and I were driving to the jetty. We would take the boat to the beach and spend the day with friends. As our car approached Falamo Bridge the traffic police waved me to the side of the road.

"Good morning, Sergeant," I said, as the policeman approached the side window that I had just lowered. "Good morning, sir. It's a hot day," he responded.

"Yes," said I. "It is a beautiful day." "It's Sunday," said

Falamo Bridge. Photo by Ilonka Hoffmanns

the policeman, hoping that I would take the hint and give him something. "Yes it is," I responded. "I really like Sundays." Since subtlety failed, the policeman tried the direct approach. "Do you have anything for me for Sunday?" he asked. Acting surprised, I looked directly at him, made the sign of the cross more or less in his general direction, and said, "Yes, I do. May the Lord's blessings be with you and your family." Flabbergasted, the policeman waved me across the bridge with a meek, "Thank you, sir."

Stuck At the Beach

By Shelley Fazzino

My three children and I were headed to the beach for a party. We loaded the car with beach towels, drinks and our food to share. Our driver, John, safely navigated the bumpy, sandy roads to arrive at the beach hut, and we enjoyed a fun time on the beach, chatting with friends and haggling with vendors.

When my sandcastle-builders grew weary, we gathered up our gear to leave. One of the village children offered assistance and thinking some money would help this small child, I allowed him to carry an empty food container 10 feet to the car. I dug in my purse and found that I had either a small or large denomination of cash to "dash" him. When I gave him the smaller bill, to my surprise, he crumpled it and threw it in my face. Shocked, I turned to John and he said, "Don't mind them."

Before I could dwell on this, John alerted me that cars were getting stuck in the ruts on the road, so we should take an alternate route to the main road. Unfortunately, we made a wrong turn and found ourselves in a remote village with only one road in. As John tried to turn around in the village, we realized our Condor was not a good vehicle to take off-road. We got stuck digging deeper and deeper in the sand.

The villagers appeared, looking to see what the commotion was about. No doubt, they were amused to see four oyibos stuck in the sand so far from home. When John asked for help, they asked for lots of naira. Well, John was not willing to sink that low even though our car was sinking in the sand, so he hopped out of the car and began rocking it. A few of the villagers assisted. I surprised John, jumping behind the wheel to steer while he desperately tried to budge the car. I wondered: are Nigerians aware that when we are not living abroad we actually drive ourselves, cook for ourselves and yes, even do our own laundry?

Despite all the pushing and shoving, we were still stuck. We pulled out our handy dandy cell phones and called a friend at the party who drives a Land Cruiser. While John went to the corner to wait for our friend's driver to arrive, my children and I waited in the car. The villagers pressed their faces against our windows and stared at us. The ridiculous nature of our predicament struck me, and I had trouble suppressing my laughter. My son asked curiously, "Why are they staring?" I explained that they probably don't see oyibos often and suggested that this is how zoo animals feel when we press our faces against their glass cages.

Soon a cavalry of six drivers appeared, and efficiently towed our car to hard ground. Before leaving, I asked John how much I should dash the villagers for their half-hearted assistance and when I gave it to them, they scoffed. I was embarrassed to be treated as a cheapskate and felt unfairly condemned as I had given them a reasonable dash. When I finally arrived home, I chalked it up to another experience in a foreign culture.

The next day we took sandwiches and drinks to the drivers in our compound who had rescued us from the sand trap. Because they were so warm and appreciative, they restored my faith in the generous, kind people of Nigeria. Despite the Nigerian proverb "It is one person in a street that kills a dog, and the street is named a street of dog killers," I'll not judge their country by a few people, because others will change my mind.

Beach vendors.
Photo by Judy Anderson

Road by the beach.
Photo by Ilonka Hoffmanns

Deaf and Dump
Anonymous

Friends and I were enjoying a day at Eleko Beach. Sitting in the shade of our hut, vendors strolled by in a steady procession like a mall going by on the sand, all the wares riding on their heads. Occasionally, a beggar would stop. One fellow had a sign that read "Deaf and Dump - Please Help". I gave the fellow some money and told his companion that the sign was misspelled.

The next week as we lounged in the hut, the two men came back with smiles and held out the sign which now read "Deaf and Damp - Please Help".

Beach vendors at Eleko Beach. Photo by Ilonka Hoffmanns

A Random Insanity?

By Gail Collins

I peeked over my shoulder snatching glances at the crammed, wriggling bodies in Bob's Bar. Where was Mick? My eyes fixed on him. Blood dripped through his fingers. Standing a thinning head of hair taller than the crowd, our friend's hawk nose coursed red. No one bothered.

"Mick's bleeding!" I yelled above the din of music, then, manoeuvred toward him, Joe in tow. Fleeing, we steered Mick to a plastic chair in the parking lot, the al fresco portion of Bob's. Ice arrived. Dutiful Joe ministered - tilt, pressure, diagnosis.

"Listen to him Mick. Joe knows what he's talking about. His brother's a doctor. His uncle's an orthopaedic surgeon. His mother's a medical transcriptionist. It's in the genes." So true. Mick's smirk suggested I was being silly. True too.

I asked the burning question, "What happened?"

Listing in his tilt to fix an eyeball on me, Mick said, "I don't know. I was just standing there, and some guy headbutted me. He's insane."

"Who's insane?"

"I don't know."

"Some Brit wearing a blue shirt?" I prompted, but Mick honestly didn't know. What did I almost remember? We bundled our friend into our car and sent him home.

* * * * * * *

Earlier, the night began as our Nigerian driver snaked the car around potholes in the road circling by the embassies where a diverse expatriate population garners assistance. The road also passes Bob's Bar, of equivalent support, nestled among other retailers. By day, the shopping complex, in various states of disrepair like Lagos itself, surrounds a car-packed lot. By night, all stands vacant, excluding a packed "Bob's Bar," its neon letters proposing happiness, generally to white patrons. Outside the periphery, dark-skinned working girls pose seductively hoping for an invitation. The slouching bouncer waved his hand at us, or maybe a fly, to enter. Not the girls.

Friday and only 9 pm. Joe and I had never seen such emptiness in Bob's, a building we joked must be a converted ship container stolen off the dock. Devoid of the crush of people, wooden flooring was discernable, clean actually. The band set up while local drinks gals leaned against the coolers awaiting the swarm. A few crepe paper streamers tacked above the polished bar pointed to a battered Happy New Year's poster signalling this Friday was different than next Friday or last Friday. The damp evening air hung waiting to be displaced by the smoke of British fags. Later. It was still early. Bob's is the place you go after you've been somewhere else. Then, you're here.

Crossing to the bar, Mick planted kisses and a squeeze on me. Not the last. He'd started his evening at home. "Gin?" I guessed licking the splashes from his glass off my arm. We didn't plan to catch up to him, yet lubrication was in order.

"Stella Artois and cider," Joe ordered. "That which doesn't kill us, makes us stronger," he recited the beer's motto. Cider, cool and dry, slaked my thirst.

Bob winked at me. Head of bar and band, the RAF Paratrooper, Korean Era, lately sported a bald head and cool shades. In fact, the bass and harmonica players were also shaved cue balls, all identifying with a mutual pal's cancer struggle. Old softies.

Cracking and whining signalled the final sound engineering feats before cranking the tunes. Mick got the nod he hopes for weekly and picked up his guitar to jam with the band until Trevor, their usual lead, showed. A snowy-bearded German, christened Saint Nick, crawled behind the cramped drum kit and these mature members began their bluesy wail. Music wrapped around us.

Fingers picked, strummed or hiked the necks of three guitars. Mick looked content, if a little glassy-eyed. A saxophone cried. The music reverberated against thin walls emblazoned with UK memorabilia - Beatles, airmen photos, band snaps and clippings hallmarking Bob's life. A sign above his head suggested, "Treachery will overcome youth every time." Perhaps.

Trevor arrived; Mick relinquished the guitar to the talented, tie-dyed dressed guy. Sidestepping microphones, dancing as the music moved through, we felt one with the band - all rock bands. Hendrix. Stones. The driving beat. The driving rain driving people inside. Jammed. Hot. Surging.

Mick drank, regularly visiting the facilities in response. Joe and I sipped, mingling the sweat of our bottles with our own as relief. When he was near, I noticed a roving hand. It reached out to make a connection. I knew whose hand it was. As fellow musicians, I chalked up the attention to the penetration of music. And alcohol. And New Year's. The fishbowl constraints of Africa plus a comfortable singing arrangement between Mick and me overshadowed his threat in a place congested to overflowing. It

153

was a party. It was a mob. The second set began.

All awareness turned to a clingy dress undulating, her pale face swinging long, dark curls. She gyrated from man to man. Grinding her teasing hips, Curls appreciated the 90% male business clientele, inevitable in hardship jobsites overseas. Plenty of attention. In a corner, the rigid body and protective glare of a young, guard-dogging Brit in a blue shirt divulged the raunchy girl's true love. New in town? I took a step. I wanted to speak to him, but the moment passed. Where was Mick? Everyone singing, dancing. The band launched straight from Neil Young into Auld Lang Syne, and then there was blood...

The band grabbed beers and joined us outside looking disgusted as we nursed Mick. It wasn't a usual night, even for Bob's Bar. My tender kiss on Mick's forehead finished him, and the rattled fellow disappeared.

But what had happened that night at Bob's? Perhaps Mick danced with Curls. Many had. We probed looking for more. Had Mick? The recollection of a Scotsman, whose callow friend planted the Glasgow kiss on Mick's face, then scooped his wife smoothly from the scene, suggested Mick had. He'd seen them dancing and hinted, "Perhaps, Mick teched her a wee bit low." I thought - perhaps youth prevailed.

Letters Home

Gems. Photo by Andrew Barton
Hyena and baboon. Photo by Katrina Head
A bit too close to the mark. Lagos Yacht Club. Photo by Andrew Barton
Kano Durbar. Photo by Bob Griffiths

The House In the Swamp

By Jo Demmer

Sent: 15 March 2005
Subject: So Here We Are in Africa!

Dear Alice,

I can't believe we have actually arrived! We have left behind the safety and familiarity of Australia for the enigma that is Nigeria.

One of our first tasks was to find a driver. I have no desire to drive here - I wouldn't survive for five minutes in the traffic. Most people find a driver through word of mouth and every staff member in the compound has a "brother" to recommend. Eventually, someone explained that Nigerians have such a strong sense of community that anyone who lives in their village is their "brother." So, you need to check whether they mean tribal brother, or someone who shares the same mother! We have been recommended a driver called Sampson whose boss is leaving soon. He is starting with us in April.

Incidentally, staff address their boss as "Master" or "Sir" and the women as "Madame" which is pronounced with the emphasis on the "d," MaDame, like the French. I find it hard not to giggle when I am called Madame, but I guess I will get used to it. So you better look out when I come home, as I will expect to be treated with deference!

Love,
Jo

Sent: 8 April 2005

Subject: A Day in the Life of a Driver

Dear Alice,

Our driver started last week. I am really pleased as he is courteous, helpful and drives safely.

You asked about what a driver does all day. His official work day is 7 am to 6 pm on weekdays and 9 am to 2 pm on Saturday. He (I say he because there are no female drivers) probably lives many miles away, and he gets up at 4:30 am for the commute to work. So it is not a surprise that he will spend some time asleep during the day - hopefully not when he is driving! Drivers are always waiting around the compound playing checkers, watching their communal TV or sleeping. I would love to sit in on some of their conversations about their Madames and Masters!

His daily duties might include driving children to school, running errands and taking Madame or Master shopping and to social or business engagements. Cleaning the car is a very serious business - ours is always impeccable inside and out. He also maintains the car, fills it with fuel and keeps the registration papers up to date.

There are hazards leaving for work before daylight; Sampson tells me that he has been mugged twice. On these occasions, he unwittingly got into a taxi which was owned by the bad guys. They grabbed his money and tossed him out. As a result, Sampson is thinking about moving closer to work. This makes sense, except of course, his rent will be more expensive. As we pay for his housing, we will no doubt be involved in this decision.

Hope you are well,

Love, Jo

Sent: 6 September 2005
Subject: Shrek

Hi there Alice,

Guess what? We are now Nigerian land owners! Well, more precisely, Sampson is, and we have become bankers! We lent Sampson money to buy a piece of land, only seven kilometres from our compound, which he will repay through salary deductions. I use the term "land" loosely, as it is really a piece of swamp! He is buying a quarter plot of land (9 m by 14 m) for the princely sum of 150,000 naira. The whole area was a swamp, but gradually people are filling it in, and now there is a whole village there. He aims to build a two-room house with a lounge and kitchen, but will start with one room and extend it as he finds the money.

When buying land in Nigeria, it is important to ensure that the vendor is the real landowner. There are horror stories about people buying land, building a house and then having the land repossessed because the proper owner turns up. To prevent this 419 (fraud), you must speak to the Bale, who is the Chief of the village. According to Sampson, the land he bought belongs to the son of the Bale. Sampson and a friend are buying a quarter plot each and will receive separate certificates of ownership. The Bale confirmed this and gave Sampson permission to buy the land. The transaction took place on Saturday.

Sampson's land is currently accessible only by wading through water between two metre high grassy reeds, so we gazed at it from afar. He told me that crabs, toads, alligators and snakes live in the swamp. This is a huge benefit, as the crabs and toads will make tasty meals and there will be great weekend entertainment alligator hunting! When I baulked at eating toads, I was told that they are delicious, whereupon I nicknamed Sampson "Shrek" - an ogre from a movie who lives in a swamp and eats toads! He thinks this is hilarious! He also explained that alligator hunting is simple; all you need is a spear as they are frightened of men and will run away. To hunt a very big alligator, he conceded it will take two men instead of one!

Stage One of Sampson's plan is to pull out all the grass and he hired men who began last Sunday. Sampson helped them in water up to mid thigh, until the workers told him more about alligators. He then decided to let the experts finish the job - so much for the brave alligator hunter!

Sampson assures me that the room will be finished by the end of November. Although we worry we might have made a monumental mistake, Sampson is a proud, new landowner.

Love,
Jo

Sent: 25 September 2005
Subject: An Update from the Swamp

Hi Alice,

The swamp land has been cleared of grass, and Stage Two, the footings, is complete. They pegged the outside of the house, and constructed the form-work for the footings out of wooden planks. These were pushed into the sand to make a frame about a foot wide. Water and sand were dug out from between the planks and replaced with iron reinforcing rods and a dry mixture of sand, cement and gravel. This absorbed the rest of the water and turned it into concrete. Along the top of

The footings and one
room filled.
Photo by Jo Demmer

Walls complete.
Photo by Jo Demmer

One room complete.
Photo by Jo Demmer

the footings were placed nine-inch cement blocks on which the walls will be constructed. Finally, after a week, the wooden form was removed and voilà - footings complete!

As usual in Nigerian building schemes, half of the essential costs were omitted from the quote, so naturally, the price has gone up. Sampson has learnt a great deal about building over the past few weeks, and so have we. For example, do not purchase any building materials until the moment they are needed and use them immediately to avoid theft. Sampson stayed up until 1:00 am guarding his footing materials before they were used. Secondly, be on site to manage the project or nothing gets done. Sampson labours alongside the workers to reduce the cost. He has decided that being a driver is infinitely easier than being a brick layer!

Now, the walls of one bedroom are going up. The inside of the footings for this room has been filled with rubble and sand to form a floor. When the roof is on, the floor and walls will be rendered in concrete. You can now access the house by walking along planks of wood that Sampson constructed into a kind of elevated footpath over the swamp.

There is no sewer or running water, so I asked about bathroom facilities. Sampson explained that he will use wooden planks to build a bathroom floor above the swamp water inside the footings for the bathroom and put iron sheets around it for privacy. They will buy a tank for water which they can refill from the village bore hole. When I ventured to ask about the murky territory of toilet waste, he cheerfully informed me that they will squat over paper, wrap it up and throw it away far into the swamp. In the dry season, he will dig a septic tank. Despite my squeamishness about this aspect of the project, it is still exciting to see the job progressing and Sampson is thrilled.

Love,
Jo

Sent: 25 November 2005
Subject: Home Sweet Home

Hi Alice,

Sampson moved into the House in the Swamp last week! It now has a roof, windows, a door and the inside is painted. It looks like a glorified "dunny block." We also decided to fill the footings for two more rooms with blocks and sand so that his children can have somewhere to play.

When Sampson started digging the foundations, he had to pay money to the Bale's sons. Work could not begin until some thousands of naira changed hands. Sampson visited the Bale to beg out of paying this fee, and he granted a concession, but Sampson still had to pay. When he put on the roof, another payment had to be made. Apparently, this is common practice.

Initially, he had no electricity, so I gave him a really thick candle for light. He couldn't believe his luck, saying that such candles are expensive in Africa. When his friends saw it, they guessed that his Madame had given it to him! It is a strange feeling to know that something so simple for us is such a delight for him.

Now, the house has electricity, courtesy of wires strung up on bamboo poles from the nearest house - all to the latest safe wiring standards of course! There is no meter box, as it is too expensive, but he is paying another man who was ordered by the Bale to share his meter box. So, there is television in the middle of the swamp! Maybe the movie Shrek will come on and give everyone a big laugh.

I went out to Sampson's Swamp several times a week to check on progress during the project. It is unusual for a white person to be seen out in the village, and Sampson says that they think I am the "site engineer!" The Bale asked whether we would like to buy some more land, but we politely declined. We have achieved our goal for Sampson, that when we leave Nigeria, regardless of whether he gets another job or not, he should always have a home for his family.

Love,
Jo

PS. 18 February, 2008
Less than a year later, the Bale was challenged by his King, who claimed to be the rightful owner of Sampson's village. He paid thugs to collect money from all property owners. Anyone who didn't comply saw their house knocked down. Women and children moved out of the area for fear of their safety. We gave Sampson this initial amount, and then, we had to wait for months while the matter was taken to court.

Eventually, the case was closed in favour of the King. He demanded that landowners pay him 2.6 million naira per plot of land. Sampson now owed 650,000 naira for the quarter-plot which he had already bought for 150,000 naira. Furthermore, they knocked down his house to construct a road through his property. In exchange, he received a quarter-plot elsewhere in the village. They rebuilt the foundation, but not the room, so Sampson had nowhere to live.

We decided not to pay for the plot, as who's to say when the next takeover will be? Who can afford to begin again and again? The amount owing has mushroomed far beyond the price of the original project. And the house needs to be rebuilt! Instead, we offered Sampson the money to rent somewhere else. So much for Sampson's land ownership.

Christmas Pudding

By Richard Perry

Hello and a big Merry Christmas to you!

It's coming up to that time of year again when everyone gets in the festive spirit for the holiday season. Well, it's no different over here in the African jungle where the palm trees become the Christmas trees and the Christmas goat is substituted for the turkey. This will be my second Christmas in Nigeria and although I will miss family, I am looking forward to it!

I came to Nigeria in August last year to the lovely little village of Eket, on the southeast coast. Sixteen months later, I have only three months to go, and I have had some amazing experiences learning about the Nigerian values and way of life.

Religion dominates here. There are more Christian churches in Eket than I can count. The missionaries did an amazing job years ago as people here believe supremely in the power of God to do "good things." On the other side, the mystical forces of bad "juju" (voodoo) haven't lost their grip.

I had an intriguing discussion with a Nigerian from work, whose wife was pregnant, regarding his expectations of being a Dad. He told me if things go well and his first born is a boy, he will bless him with a religious name, like Chukwuemeka, which means "God has done well." In the unfortunate event the child is a girl (not something the man seriously considered) he would wait a few months before naming her, and probably not give her a blessed name (sorry, ladies). Not that we discussed it at the time, but if something went horribly wrong, like death, there is no "God had a reason for it." Anything bad like that initiates cries of "Bad Juju!" Out comes the python oil and other tribal medicines that exorcise evil curses from grieving mothers. Discovering these sorts of rites is interesting, if sometimes disturbing, but I am certainly earning a broader perspective on life.

My final three-month stint will be based mainly in the city of Lagos where I have quite a different lifestyle. An estimated 25 million people are crammed into this city spread over the mainland and islands connected by bridges, but if you saw the camping and swamp-style housing, in addition to the people forever on the move or clinging to life on a bridge pylon, you'd realize the population figures are just a guesstimate. The drawback to Lagos is traffic, with hour commutes covering only 10 kilometers alongside too many other cars that choke the air with smog. On the upside, there are thousands more expats here with activities crowding the weekends.

On Saturday I played in a company-sponsored softball tournament at AISL. The event hosted six teams including one comprised of half of the national women's softball team! We had a brilliant day with our team coming in second and Cajun prawns at the party afterwards. In the evening, I went to a Christmas party, and then I rolled out of bed on Sunday to relax the afternoon away at a beach hut with a fellow Aussie. We ate prawns and fresh fish, drank a few beers and swam in the sea surrounded by dozens of laughing little African boys staring at us as we got dumped by the short, breaking waves.

My plans for Christmas involve a return to Eket and a road trip to Obudu Cattle Ranch. A few of us, including our friend, the local security guy, will pile into a car and drive about six to eight hours north. Contrary to the name, there are apparently few, if any, cattle at the ranch. Its mountain landscape should be a change from the tropical 30° to 40° Celsius we normally sweat through, and animal life is more abundant. Not the usual types you think of, so don't worry, Mum - no lions and rhinos - but there are monkeys, birds and other small jungle species. I'll even have to pack a jumper (sweater for the Yanks) as it's technically winter at the moment, and with the elevation, it could be up to 20 degrees cooler. It will be a nice change.

My group of friends is sticking to tradition this year, and we plan a turkey and Christmas pudding! An Aussie mate who loves to haggle for local produce will gather the local fruits and berries and make a Nigerian Christmas pudding. Yours Truly is responsible for the bird, and I was surprised to find a turkey farmer in town. I negotiated a price and delivery of the bird for December 24 and walked away with a big smile of satisfaction. I turned back and asked the farmer, a semi-naked man with a three-foot machete in hand, politely of course, "How will the turkey be delivered?" His reply, translated from Pidgin English, "Under my arm on the back of a motorbike, live and kicking!" So, my Christmas turkey saga is far from over as I try to convert a full-size gobbler into the neat, plastic-wrapped package that Mum buys from the supermarket. I may end up with a pet turkey and no Christmas dinner... Ah, the adventure of life in Nigeria!

I've met some amazing people here, both local and expat. I've traveled, run about 20 Hashes (jungle bush bash runs), eaten some new and unusual food (such as white clay - a local source of calcium - and "bush meat," which is the hunter's daily catch from the jungle) and I was crowned a Junior Chief in a special ceremony. I hope you are well wherever you happen to be in the world, and I wish you all the best for Christmas and the New Year. And as you sit down to your Christmas dinner and slice your delicious turkey, spare a thought for me and what it takes to get a Christmas turkey here in Africa!

Cheers,

Rich

Jingle Bells
By Martha Peterson

Christmas was approaching and a Kindergarten class was learning about Christmas carols. The teacher wrote the words to Jingle Bells on the blackboard.

"Dashing through the snow, In a one horse open sleigh…"

She asked the eager children in front of her "Who can tell me what 'dashing' means?" Ten hands shot up in the air. The teacher selected a boy and he confidently suggested "That's when you pay Nigerians for doing something."

Caroling, Caroling

By Les Johnson

Les, Zdenka, Jurgen and Shirley laughed happily as their driver sped through the streets of Lagos after a late night Christmas party. For so few people on the road, there were, however, an inordinate number of roadblocks with police checking papers, asking for money, and generally, threatening their gay mood.

So, the two couples began to sing. Lagos is a cosmopolitan place with no shortage of nationalities, and this car had a representative sampling: Croatian, Canadian, Scottish and German. The singers belted out "We Wish You a Merry Christmas!" in their native tongues and distinct vocal ranges. This cacophony of sound seemed to work as they made their way through four roadblocks without a hassle.

Then, at the last one, the policeman asked them to open the car door. We're in trouble now, they thought. The policeman surprised them by smiling as he shook their hands thanking them for the song.

Let's Talk Turkey

By Marionette Audifferen

I'll never forget our first Christmas in Nigeria. My husband received a turkey as a corporate gift. A live turkey. He's originally from Nigeria, so you'd think he would remember such spectacular details as giving live animals as gifts. Apparently, Ade's recall had dulled from too many trips to American grocery stores where pristine meat counters house innocuous, non-animated breasts and drumsticks.

His memories woke with a shock as he witnessed an office security guard wrestling a live turkey into his car that December evening. Arriving home with the turkey, our four children delighted in their new pet, until they discovered its intended journey was our Christmas dinner table. Then, they shrieked with horror, vowing not to eat the turkey if we killed it.

Well, Christmas was still on the horizon, so we let the big guy have the run of the compound. Three days later, the turkey had pooped over so much of our yard that we all begged our cook to kill it and roast it. Gobble, gobble means a tasty turkey dinner for Christmas in our house now.

Christmas Blessings

By Kathy Eckert

Merry Christmas from Lagos, Nigeria!

We hope this finds you happy, healthy and enjoying a wonderful Christmas season celebrating the birth of our Saviour. We can't believe we've been in Nigeria for a year and a half already. Let us tell you how Christ has blessed us in this fascinating land of wonder and brokenness.

While we lament giving up our big house in Texas, our Nigerian neighbors feel blessed because they have an 8x8 foot room to house their family and in some cases extended family as well. We gain much from their satisfaction.

We miss all our favorite foods from the States, but still have a pantry and freezer overflowing with so many choices. The biggest blessing is ours when we bring a plateful of leftover dinner to one of our guards and receive the most sincere grin and a "God Bless You." We guess that this is all he has eaten today.

We are blessed because we have clean water to drink and power most of the time (thanks to back up generators). Our driver is happy when he gets six hours of sleep on the occasion the power is on to run his fan and cool the 95 degree night. Most never have power.

We are blessed to have a roof that doesn't leak too badly. That we have a roof at all.

We are blessed that we have a steady income, well above the

poverty line, and do not need to use it to support four or five families.

We are blessed that we have a means of transportation, a refrigerator and a choice of what to wear each day.

We are blessed that for our children, who accrued 30,000 frequent flyer miles last year, the world is their play ground, while our housekeeper has never been anywhere but to her village and this island where she lives near us in "the quarters."

We are blessed to watch the boys from the village laughing with glee while playing soccer with a ball of rags. Our children complain about practising for their music lessons, or tennis, or a multitude of other activities they are "forced" to do.

We are blessed that our legs aren't crippled from polio, that our arms are not amputated and that when we were hit with illnesses and two broken arms last year, we had access to a doctor.

Our challenge to you this season is to celebrate and enjoy, but mostly to count one blessing each day. God is good! All the time! Even in Nigeria!

We love you and miss you,

Jeff, Kathy, Jared, Ryan and Anna Grace

Helping Others

Gems. Photo by Els Van Limberghen
School teacher at Ishahayi Beach. Photo by Shelley Fazzino
Carpenter at work at Ishahayi Beach. Photo by Jeff Eckert
School children at Cardoso. Photo by Gail Collins

Miracles Happen

By Ilonka Hoffmanns

It was just another sunny day in Lagos. The streets were filled with the sounds of honking cars and humming air conditioners. I did not know yet, but it was a day that would change my life. I was driving to an orphanage to give a medical check to four children who had arrived two days ago. As a nurse for the adoption agency, I examined all children in our adoption procedure. At the orphanage I saw a playground with a sand floor. The swings and slides looked old, but in good condition. Around the playground was a low, U-shaped building. No children were playing with the toys outside, but I heard lots of children's voices.

Inside, the nannies were busy washing and feeding the children. They pointed out the four new ones; a darling five-month-old boy, a cute three-month-old boy and a beautiful 15-month-old girl, all in very good health. Where was Child Number Four? Hannah? In a bed lay an 18-month-old girl, so skinny that I could not believe my eyes. She wore a dress that was four sizes too big. She was constantly sucking on her fingers. Tears welled up in my eyes. How could a child become so skinny? What had happened to her? Hannah's skin was very hot, and I realized she had a high fever. I picked her up and was surprised that she weighed less than the three-month-old baby I had just held in my arms.

I quickly took Hannah to the hospital fearing that she would not live very long if we waited. She weighed four kilos (eight and a half pounds). The fever had made Hannah dehydrated. That, together with malaria and chronic diarrhea, had brought Hannah to the edge. We could only hope that we were not too late.

The next day, her fever had gone. I arranged to foster her in my home to nurse her back to health. This was my personal dream come true - to look after an orphaned child. I was not experienced in nursing malnourished children and I thought that it was a matter of love and food to heal her. Little did I know the ordeal that lay ahead to get Hannah healthy!

My children were delighted to have a baby sister. They hugged and kissed her and showed her photo at school. Hannah quickly became more alert. She was obviously responding to our love.

The fontanel on top of her head was still open, while normally this closes by the age of one. The late closure of her fontanel could indicate that she had been sick since she was a few months old. The biggest problem in Hannah's treatment was to get rid of the chronic diarrhea. All our love and care did not help this. She did not drink enough to balance the loss of fluid and vital minerals. I constantly worried that she could have heart failure. As she was so skinny, no diapers fit her; they all left a big opening around her legs where watery stool dripped through. We changed her six times a day.

After a week, the loss of fluid became too much. A blood test showed that Hannah was very low in potassium. This could cause heart failure at any moment, so we rushed to the hospital, 45 minutes away. I sat down in the ambulance with Hannah and constantly spoke to her. "Hang on Sweetie. Know that a beautiful life with loving adoptive parents is waiting for you. You have a bright future. Grab it!"

Finally at the hospital, I tried to answer the long list of admission questions. Already at the first question there was a difficulty. What is Hannah's surname? I did not know. As she had to have a surname, we gave her ours. The second question was the name of the mother. Again, I had no answer. It had to be mine then. Same for the father and so, within 10 minutes we became Hannah's parents on paper. Many questions were left unanswered, and it made me feel sorry for Hannah. She did not have a past on paper.

Hanna was admitted. Lynn, my children's nanny, stayed in the hospital with her to comply with hospital requirements. The room looked gloomy. It was old, the air conditioner did not work and the windows let a stream of warm, humid air into the room. I had packed a simple bag with diapers, clothes for Hannah and her cuddly toy. Lynn wrote a long list of things for me to bring on my next visit, and I was surprised to learn that this hospital had virtually nothing. I had to bring a bowl, cutlery, cups, food for Hannah and Lynn, bed sheets, towels, soap, shampoo and bottled water.

Hannah was put on one of the two beds. There were no side railings, so Hannah could fall out. She looked so vulnerable in this big bed. I hugged her and left. On the way home, I could only think of one thing: that she would survive all this.

She did very well in hospital. The diarrhea stopped, and she finally gained some weight. After four days we were happy to bring her back home. We thought we had beaten the diarrhea, but as soon as we were home, it recurred. Was it a reaction to the medication? She was given antibiotics by drip in hospital. At home we had to give it to her orally, and she did not like it.

Hannah was now part of our family, and we took her everywhere with us. One Saturday, we took Hannah to the Lagos Yacht Club. She sat on my lap, and suddenly, I heard a lot of gas expelled from her little body. I knew it was not just gas, so I lifted her up to check, only to see that it had all dripped on my skirt. I was covered in poop. It was time to go home.

Hannah became weak again. She had more dirty diapers than she would drink, and it was beginning to show. My oldest daughter got the flu and was quite sick. She passed it on to Hannah, who could not handle it and became dehydrated in just one day. She just lay there, weak, sleepy and not present in this world. Her temperature was very low, but she felt like a burning oven. Alarm bells went off in my head and we rushed her to the hospital again. She was balancing between life and death. There was no time to wait for the ambulance. Lynn held Hannah on her lap. A tiny thin arm stuck out of the blanket. It was only as thick as my thumb.

The traffic was heavy. It took 90 long minutes to reach the hospital. As we did not arrive by ambulance, they were not expecting us, and we had to wait for a very long time. I was agitated. I walked up and down the hall in search of a nurse to help us, but it seemed they were all too busy.

Finally, I found a nurse and urged her to hurry as we had a dying child here. The nurse took Hannah's temperature, gave her a paracetamol and then brought us to a tired-looking doctor. His half-opened eyes looked at me, pointing to sit down. Lynn still had Hannah in her arms. "What is the problem, Madam?" he asked, completely ignoring the child. "What is the problem?" I said a bit loudly back to him. Could he not see? We came here with a dying child. Do something! He shrugged his shoulders.

"Relax Madam, we see many children like this. Is this not the child we released just a week ago? In GOOD HEALTH?" Was he accusing me of neglecting this child? With my nerves already balancing on despair, I asked him with an icy voice, "Why don't you have a look at the child? That is what you are supposed to do!"

He looked at me and rang a bell for a nurse to come and help him. I felt ashamed for my behavior, but I was so upset about Hannah. While the doctor was examining Hannah, I looked at his desk and noticed a small army of tiny ants walking around. Ants were everywhere and considered part of the interior. The doctor announced that Hannah had a fever and said "Nurse, give her a cold bath." I protested. Hannah had already been given a paracetamol to lower her fever. A cold bath could have a devastating effect on her weak heart.

They took Hannah to the bathroom and poured cold water on my skinny girl. I could have cried. I was so afraid she would die that I asked the nurse to stop. She asked me for a towel. They did not have towels? Oh, I forgot. I lost my patience and with a strong voice I said, "What is this hospital where you treat children but have no towels?" I grabbed the towel we had brought, telling myself to behave. I was being unreasonable because I loved Hannah so much. The bath had done her good, and the fever was dropping. They admitted her, and Lynn stayed with her.

A week went by, and Hannah improved. She gained weight, grew strong enough to sit up and was ready to come home. Our children were happy to have their foster sister back. We enjoyed her very much.

Two days later, I found something beside Hannah on her bed that looked like a white rolled-up elastic band. What was it? I gave it a closer look and realized in horror, it was a worm! Where had it come from? Her nose? I took it to the doctor, and he gave Hannah a de-worming treatment. This had been the source of the recurring diarrhea all along. Another worm was removed, and from that moment on, Hannah was on the way to the top.

Hannah got stronger and stronger. She started crawling and her behaviour developed from that of a very young baby to that of a one-and-a-half-year-old. People were surprised to see her growing so big. They told me that they had not trusted her to live. Hannah was loved by everyone in our compound. The Nigerian workers always called her name when they saw her with me. Some told me they envied her for being adopted and having the opportunity for a good future. Other Nigerian people were only pleased to see an oyibo with a black baby. "You black baby. Very good, very good!"

Hannah has since been adopted by Dutch parents and lives a happy life in Holland. She survived. Miracles happen!

So Sorry

By Marzuki Abdul Jabar

Suffering from a sore throat, I was waiting to see a doctor at the medical clinic. My throat began to tickle, and a coughing spasm erupted as my body tried to dislodge the irritants thriving in my throat. As I coughed, a cleaning lady passed by and said, "So sorry." I looked up at her, and she repeated her gesture, "So sorry."

To avoid looking rude, I said, "Thank you," and smiled, wondering why she had apologized to me. I was the one sending my germy microbes airborne through a public place.

The thought and confusion resurfaced at my next clinic visit when my daughter needed to have a wound cleaned. A Nigerian woman saw it and said, "So sorry."

I asked a Nigerian colleague why people say "So sorry" to someone, even a complete stranger, who is sick or injured. He said that it is customary to say this to express sympathy in the hope that this gesture will help the sick person to feel better. In what I usually consider a trying work location, this simple act of caring truly touched me.

A Visit to the Ikoyi Jail

By Lindy Edwards

What started as a usual Monday morning took an interesting turn. I left home in Ikoyi to spend several hours at the Motherless Babies Home in Alapere-Ketu, run by the Sisters of Mother Theresa. Usually, I feed and change the babies, cuddle and read to the toddlers and conduct some activities for the two and three year-olds such as coloring and teaching numbers. I visit here twice a week and enjoy my contact with the children. The Sisters and novices at the home do a wonderful job, but any extra help is appreciated.

This particular morning, at about 10 am, Sister Lourdes (Mother Superior) asked if she could borrow my driver and vehicle. The nuns and some volunteers had been awake all night preparing food for the 2500 prisoners in the Ikoyi jail. Individual portions of rice and meat had been packed into plastic bags and there were 2500 oranges. The truck to transport the food had not arrived and it was getting late. So, we loaded the food into the Sisters' van and my Land Cruiser. Both were packed full and their flattened tires revealed their heavy loads. I sat with three nuns in their vehicle and my driver and guard traveled with a male member of the parish in our vehicle.

It was my first visit to a jail in Nigeria, so I was a little apprehensive and keen to observe everything closely. The entrance to the jail consisted of two gates. When we arrived, we were waved through the first gate, with the second still closed, and Sister told me to remain in the vehicle while she signed in.

Both vehicles were then admitted and we drove along a dirt path directly to the chapel inside the jail. Sister stressed that mobile phones were not permitted and demonstrated the example by switching hers off.

The prisoners were in the grounds washing clothes, washing themselves, kicking a football or just sitting around. They looked lean and muscular, evidence that their food supplies were adequate and fitness was important. I looked around wondering what crimes these men had committed. The buildings I saw were single-storied and in my brief glimpse, they appeared to be randomly placed throughout the grounds. Although the term "boys' camp" came to mind, this is too flippant to depict the tragedy of men's lives wasted inside these walls for up to 15 years.

The nuns were warmly welcomed, and our band of helpers walked into the simple chapel where we were shown to seats behind the wooden altar. Hymns were sung, prayers said and Mother Superior addressed the 300 prisoners. Although I couldn't hear what she said, the prisoners were captivated by her words and presence.

After this hour-long service we left the chapel to unload the food. One of the prison-guards, wielding a cane stick as his only weapon, said that the food should be distributed outside the chapel, not in God's house. After a few words by one of the nuns, the food was taken inside! The two vehicles were then asked to leave the prison to wait for us outside. On previous visits, the nuns had handed the food to each prisoner, but due to our late arrival, the cell captains collected food for their cellmates. With a guard marking off a list, cell captains came into the chapel carrying buckets or Hessian bags and were given anywhere from 40 to 150 food packages as appropriate. The cell captains were quiet and respectful, and the choir sang during all this time. My guard, who is a preacher when he is off duty, was excellent, never moving more than a few feet away from me. Whilst I was conscious of being in a jail it was not a threatening environment.

After handing out the food, it was time to leave and we all walked back to the double-gated entrance. The nuns and I, being female, just walked out. However our male cohorts needed to show authorization to prove they were not inmates before they were allowed out!

Driving home, the discussion between my driver, guard and me focused on what we had just experienced. When faced with the poverty in Lagos, to see those who don't even have their own freedom was confronting. In a sorry way, some of these men were probably better fed and clothed in the jail than outside. All the same, freedom is invaluable. What started as a normal day took a diversion and certainly left me thinking...

Little Trucks Coming and Going

By Marla Kunfermann

My sharpest childhood memory is of my grandmother standing in front of her gas stove, begging, beseeching and sometimes demanding that God give her the strength to pull up a chair and stick her head inside. In adulthood, my mantra became "don't let me be like Grandma, please don't let me be like Grandma." So imagine my surprise a few years ago, when I moved from Lagos to Ikot Abasi, Akwa Ibom State to a project camp surrounded by an eight-foot chain link fence topped with Stalag 17 razor wire, and I nearly became my grandmother!

In the beginning, everyday was a battle of black depression, and I suddenly understood the siren call of an unlit burner. Not that I would have chosen the stove as my way out of this "veil of tears." Oh no, nothing so PASSIVE for me, winner of Most Flamboyant in my 7th Grade class. My plan was much more diabolical. I would lie behind the wheels of my husband's Jeep and wait for him to back out on his predawn journey to the job site. This would ensure that Ernst agonized over his active participation in my final departure for the rest of his life. Hopefully, each time he backed out of a driveway, he would say to himself sadly, with a little tear in the corner of his eye, "Marla was a good wife, I really should have gotten her out of that camp!"

My mood didn't last long. Years before we married, Ernst had spent time in a camp, and he knew that "life in a golden cage" as he always referred to it, could make a person crazy. He watched me like a hawk and did all the right things to keep me away from the oven: bought me a car, designed a fishpond and arranged road trips.

One of my favorite Igbo proverbs says, "When a cow is born without a tail, God will swish his flies." And this was true in my life. It turned out that my time spent behind the wire was, on the whole, very happy - good friends, interesting activities and trips impossible to take from Lagos. One outing led me to my cook's village. He wanted to hook me up with a "starving artist," literally so the man appeared, although I did not realize the severity of it at the get-go.

Art Friday (I christened him this to avoid confusion with Friday Cook and Friday Driver) was actually a sign writer. On that first visit, I stepped out of his mud hut and over the most incredible crucifix lying on the ground. Two-feet long and fashioned from cast concrete, it was meant to adorn a mausoleum. It was beautiful in both design and detail, although I must admit, Christ had a strangely unnerving look about the eyes as he gazed, not heavenward, but at his own crown of thorns - a circlet of rusty nails.

I asked Art Friday how he had made it. First, he carved the negative image into the ground, pounded hard by years of bare feet. Then he poured the concrete in and let it harden. After digging it out, he rubbed it with sand to produce a smooth finish.

Forget the sign writing, I knew we were on to something unique, something truly exceptional. And that is how Art Friday and I went into the garden statuary business. After trying a few different designs, my favorite items were the three-foot-tall garden gnomes. A cross between the Menny Hoonies of Hawaii and the fertility deities of West Africa, everybody thought they looked a bit too phallic to have sitting around the yard. In fact one night, for lack of a chair on our patio, I perched atop one. When Ernst finally focused on the total picture, he said, "Marla, get off that thing. It looks like you're sitting on a giant penis!" So much for garden gnomes.

Art Friday and I finally decided on elephants. Believe it or not, this was a frustrating endeavor. The first elephant had a horse's tail and lion's feet, complete with two-penny nails for the claws (Art Friday hated to waste building materials and always looked to recycle leftovers). The next model had the tail right, but sported cloven hoofs. Was this passive aggression? Did he not want to work for a woman? Finally I asked him, what the deal was - could he not just sculpt an elephant?

"Madame," he explained, "I have never seen an elephant, and this is what my family has decided one would look like." Hellooooo Marla? How long had I lived here? Ten-plus years? Had I seen any elephants lumbering through the mangrove swamp? Well, neither had he. We solved the problem with children's books featuring elephants in every possible pose and came up with a really good design: one compact piece with nothing to break off or poke out, making them easy to transport and eventually ship.

Each elephant was hand-sculpted in red mud, then coated with a concrete skin where finer details were worked straight onto the wet cement. I was always astounded when after saying "this needs to be broader" or "he needs a fold in his ear about here," Art Friday could whip out a bent butter knife and flick this, jab that, or shave there to achieve the perfect effect. When it hardened, Art Friday chipped a hole in the side to dig out the mud with a sharp stick, then repaired the wound. This was slow going, so as the business took off, he designed a five-piece mold where individual pieces of a 3-D puzzle were "glued" together with cement. This idea bordered on genius.

When I was young, a family friend constantly schemed up money-making ideas, and whenever something was in the works, he said he was on his way to having "little trucks coming and going." We indeed had trucks coming and going, Ernst's company trucks. But so much heavy traffic completely broke down the road to the village. So, Ernst diverted his company laborers out to the bush and rebuilt an entire road for transportation of cement and the finished elephants. We sent these amazing elephants all over the world: Spain, Switzerland, Germany, Canada, the U.S and Kenya. But how could we ensure they got there in one piece? Packers from the local branch of a worldwide shipping company developed a box sturdy enough, and with our little trucks smoothly coming and going, we finally named our business *Elephant Walk*.

One day a frantic Art Friday turned up at our door. The police had noticed all those trucks coming and going, and upon investigation, they found our field of garden elephants. They reported us to the tax authorities who threatened to smash every one unless we paid our bills at the White House - the local tax office quartered in an old house painted white. The paperwork of our formally-recognized business became madness.

I truly loved it all, even the numerous hour-and-a-half-long trips to the village to take care of the minutia of running a business. The village is hidden away, so Friday Cook navigated for Friday Driver around every bend. Moreover, they chatted with each other and argued over religion. I would put on my earphones and pretend I couldn't hear them, but it would have taken a deaf man not to hear them.

I joined in one day when Friday Driver said he knew exactly how old he was because his father had taken the trouble to record the births of his children. Friday Cook, on the other hand, was not quite sure of the year he was born. I asked him how he could figure it out, and he talked about living without a calendar. Daily life was measured in days before and after Market Day. In the old days, Before Before, a mother noted which field was planted with groundnuts when her baby was born. When a different crop was planted there, her child would be four years old, and in another cycle, he would be eight. Crop rotation, however, had no bearing on when a child was the right age to go to school. Old enough was when he could reach an arm over his head and touch his ear.

Landmarks also denoted time in village life: flood, famine, fire, and government changeover. Cook Friday said, "We used to count every Big Thing by outbreaks of Small Pox, but when we successfully prayed out Small Pox, we could no longer use it as a time marker." I asked, "What do you mean you prayed out Small Pox?" And he solemnly replied, "Prayer Warriors gathered and prayed for days." He continued, "After many days, some doctors came from America to ask if we had Small Pox. We said, 'Yes,' and they vaccinated us. Prayer brought them to us, and we never had Small Pox in the village again. We prayed Small Pox away." I think about this quite often and consider not just the power of prayer, but the power of believing prayer is powerful.

Every time I went out to the village, I saw improvements that Art Friday had provided for his family or the entire village.

His old mother was the village palm oil woman. She rendered the oil from the ripe kernels by tying the ends of a sheet around two hefty sticks and getting little boys to twist the sheet between them, hand over hand, literally wringing the palm oil out. Exhausting work even for energetic kids, they did it in tag teams and most of the children in the village had biceps you could strike a match on. One of the first things Art Friday bought was a wooden press like those used for cider, grapes or olives. Even as his mother's workload went down, her production went up.

Art Friday also bought a radio so everybody could listen to news and sports. The village had no electricity, though poles marched right through to the next town, and since batteries were expensive, they solved the problem by climbing the pole and connecting the radio cord right into the lines.

It was all good news. Art Friday's children now attended school complete with books and uniforms, and his hut had a new roof. His wife became a trader, as did a sister or two. He even employed a brother. But most striking was Art Friday's health. When I met him, my starving artist had been suffering from TB, and I had mistaken his thin frame and hollow eyes for a poor diet. He was very nearly a Dying Artist. With his increased fortunes, Art Friday was able to pay for medication which restored his health.

Elephant Walk boomed for five years before Ernst and I were called back to the States. I was not sure when, or even if, we would return to Nigeria. One thing was sure, Art Friday's business could not last without us. Ernst's trucks and road repair were essential, and I organized the books, paid the taxes, managed sales and advertising, plus arranged for shipping worldwide. I didn't see how it could keep going if we left extendedly. It would surely come apart. Still, we had to leave.

I organized a huge Goodbye Party in the village, but I was too upset to enjoy it. I hated to think of Art Friday's children without school fees and his aging mother working harder to help. And it hurt me that they might think I was leaving them, like they didn't matter, for my new life, when in reality, the hours spent with these villagers were some of my most memorable. I wanted them to like me.

While I sat somberly, they swilled Coca Cola and squabbled over cookies. Children clacked new spoons on new cups, wide-eyed babies gurgled and goats stamped around like they had at every other party we had held. Did they not realize that this was the last one? That literally, their party was over?

Art Friday and I sat on a stump, and I told him I was sorry that this would be the end for Elephant Walk. And then he said something that has stayed with me ever since, "Madam if I never make another Kobo from this business, it is OK because in this time, I have been truly blessed. I have health now and my mother has a palm press. If anything happens to me, she can support herself. And my children realize education is important, so they will work hard to get more. None of this could have happened without this business. But if it is over, I will be happy with what I have from it. I cannot ask for more."

It took me a minute to realize he was sincere. It was so un-American. I had been dreaming of bigger and better. Nothing had ever been enough. I wanted those little trucks to keep coming and going with *Elephant Walk* emblazoned on both sides. I sat with a cup of warm coke, bitterly disappointed, while beside me, Art Friday sat, enjoying the same warm coke, his health, his mother's independence and every single thing he had accomplished with a bent butter knife and a patient hand.

I think about it all to this day. Little thoughts coming and going.

Short End of the Stick

By Lee McKee

Ray, an expat rotator for an oil company, winced at the pitiful rush brooms the locals used to tidy up the rig. Bent over the two-foot broom, the sweeping looked painful and inefficient. On his return flight from home leave, Ray hand-carried a modern miracle, long-handled, dust-catcher of a broom. He presented it to the cleaner who beamed with joy. The next day, keen to see his present in action, Ray peeked around a corner to catch sight of his friend doubled over having cut the long handle off to suit his habits.

Cardoso

By Gail Collins

As fifteen women piled out of the van and cars at Cardoso Catholic Community Project on St. Mary's Church grounds at Ajegunle, the Sisters embraced them like old friends. We'd never met, but to the Sisters, the AWC extends an ongoing hand of friendship and support, so the embrace was natural. Wanda Devlin directed this field trip for members to witness the concrete successes of training, caring and contributions. We did not expect such a humbling shower of affections and respect.

Sr. Mary Akinwale, Project Coordinator, introduced the Board members and gave a synopsis of the "Mustard Seed" concept of Cardoso. Established in 1973 by Rev. Sr. Helena Brennan, its goal is to help the less privileged executing its motto of "Empowerment for Life." The project inspiration came after the Civil War of 1970 to help combat the high rate of unemployment, lack of social control and police protection, poverty, crime, unstable homes and need for stimulation by illiterate villagers seeking work. AWC's involvement began with the project's inception. A flat in Pa Cardoso's house became a base for the sisters to plan, fund and organize. From four pioneering students, the facility grew steadily to comprise five major areas: Vocational Secondary School, Multi-Purpose Unit (including Library, Employment Office, Adult Literacy and Counseling areas), Women's Training Center, Primary Health Clinic and Play Center/Nursery.

Leaving the Sister's Residence to begin the tour, Sr. Mary waved her arm wide across the spacious grounds saying, "This is all filled to overflowing from church on Sunday." St. Mary's Catholic Church is separate from Cardoso, but acts as a conducive venue - a vibrant place of positive activity. At the Secondary School, the group met students dressed in uniforms of yellow and ochre keeping beat with a step and literally singing AWC's praises and their thanks. A tiny girl in blue and beads presented a flower bouquet. Community support is evident and much appreciated.

In the Multi-Purpose Units, students worked on the ten available computers, some donated by Halliburton. One girl created a changing screen of welcome and thanks to the group. The typing lab hummed with the rhythmic click of manual typewriters donated by AWC. Around the campus, signs on buildings and equipment displayed the names of supporting oil companies, churches, Lions and Rotary Clubs and commemorated events like Year of the Child.

The Administrator of the Women's Training Center, Sister Julianne, introduced us to five classes studying sewing, handwork and cookery skills. Each room displayed their practicals, or handiwork. The two-year program currently enrolls 280 students. The girls buy their own material and thread to learn to crochet, embroider and sew clothes by hand and treadle machine. In a kitchen with seven ovens, four were broken, but the functioning three baked scrumptious meat pies that had our stomachs rumbling, and icing crowned three cakes slated for a Saturday wedding.

The Clinic employs 25 staff in a laboratory, treatment area, dispensary, four consulting rooms, feeding class and Nursery/ Play Center. A poster stating "Health is Wealth" sums up the results of Cardoso's education, immunization programs, counseling, daycare, treatment of disease (including HIV), family planning, antenatal well-care, nutritional guidance and charity extended to those unable to pay.

A peek into the Play Center stopped the youngest children in their coloring or lessons. They eagerly sang of their happiness in going to school and voiced thanks in unison. The two-year olds clapped their hands and cheered, "When you're happy and you know it, say 'Welcome.'" Our smiles mirrored theirs. We felt very welcome.

A consistent power source at Cardoso is nearly nonexistent due to an unreliable generator, but a donation of 750,000 naira from the American International School in Lagos and matched by AWC will address this soon. Multi-pronged support allows Cardoso to offer families, who otherwise couldn't afford to pay for a daughter's education, a chance to break the continuing cycle of untrained and unemployable women. A sliding scale enhanced by scholarship money keeps the project viable. That morning Wanda presented Sr. Mary with 94,000 naira collected from AWC members to clear loan debts for a number of underfinanced girls.

The tour concluded with an invitation to sit under the mango tree to relax and enjoy a presentation. The staff brought minerals, fruit, a cake and the meat pies we'd smelled cooking to assure us they were "highly grateful." The event commenced with prayer, song, comedy skit and traditional dance. The dancing revealed passion and storytelling. Many of the visitors spoke later of the thrill of being included in an authentic Nigerian experience and celebration. Further, the students' consistent pride in Nigeria impressed and moved us. During part of the show, a group of students sang and stepped to the beat, taking turns to address a verse to us. One chanted of their joy at Cardoso with "The Garden - Our parents planted the seeds, and AWC waters them. God raises us up. We will not disappoint you." Such a privilege to be in their midst. From a tiny mustard seed of desperate need in 1973, a large tree with many branches grows 30 years later.

Dancing at Cardoso. Photo by Gail Collins

Why Am I Here?

By Andrew Barton

Why am I here?

I came here for the expatriate payroll, it's true,
But I am here for many other reasons, too.

I came here for the corporate kudos from working in a "hard-to-staff" location,
Yet I realise how lucky I am to have any job that provides a regular income.

I came here for the challenge of working in an environment that tests your resolve to make a difference,
Yet I am rewarded for simple things such as making a guard's day by giving him a packet of biscuits.

I came here because it is exciting to work in an industry that is experiencing tremendous growth and prosperity,
Yet it is frustrating and disappointing to see that these benefits appear to bypass the masses of people living below the poverty line.

I came here to enjoy the luxuries of an expatriate lifestyle,
Yet I witness the brutality of life where just feeding the family each day is a triumph.

I came here for the opportunity to travel the world and visit lands both familiar and foreign,
Yet just living here is more of an adventure than any vacation in the developed world.

I came here to experience life in one of the world's most populous countries,
Yet this heightens my appreciation for growing up in one of the world's least populous countries.

I came here to learn about a very different social culture,
Yet I find that the fundamentals of humanity are universal.

I came here for the international friendships offered by an expatriate community,
Yet I enjoy a stronger sense of patriotism with my fellow countrymen here than I ever experienced in my home country.

I came here to improve the future prospects and quality of life for my family and me,
Yet I am presented with endless opportunities to improve the quality of life for the Nigerians that I meet - it is my privilege to help build a school in a remote fishing village, where education offers the children of Ishahayi Beach the opportunity for a better future.

Why am I here?

By living in Nigeria, I have discovered why I am here.

Epilogue

Time's Up

By Jo Demmer

I sit beside the plane window watching the endless shanties of Lagos disappear beneath me. It is a hazy vision, blurred by silent tears coursing down my face.

Smiling through my tears, I remember the first time I flew into Lagos, full of dread and apprehension; moving to a country I knew little or nothing about except fear-mongering news reports. I think of the research I did on health risks such as malaria and security risks - had I gone crazy to agree to such a place, as some of my friends suggested? I sought adventure, but was afraid to take the first plunge. Could that really have been just three years ago?

The plane engines whir in my ears and I try to be lulled out of my sadness. I think of the times during my stay when I was so ready to leave. Tired from the small frustrations when it seemed that everything was just too hard. Tired of the traffic. Tired of living with fear hovering in the background. Then one day, my husband came home from work and said, "Time's up. We're being sent home." And my world stopped.

I think of saying goodbye to my friends and the tears flow more freely. Connections had been forged that were hard to release. How do you say goodbye to staff who have become part of the family, who have cooked for you, driven you, played with your children and eagerly taught you so much about their culture? How do you say goodbye to friends who have shared so much, both fun and fraught with angst, that you feel you have proverbially walked through fire together?

My son sees my tears and asks, "Mummy, why are you crying?" I say, "Sometimes, it's hard to say goodbye." He replies, "Yes I know." He too, had been sad to leave - our pool, our compound, his school, his friends. Then he adds, "But Mum, we're going home." "You're right." I say and hug him.

I am excited about reuniting with friends and family. But there is trepidation here too - will I fit back in? Or will I feel like a pregnant woman who finds that her feet have grown and her old, comfortable shoes no longer fit? I know life's challenges will not end now that I have left, but I will face new ones, different ones. Back in my real world.

Although, life never felt more real than when I lived in Lagos. Nigeria was my world and my home too. It is hard to imagine that I might not ever go there again. And I realise, there's a small part of me I've left behind, and there's something I've brought with me that will be mine forever.

Footprints

By Gail Collins

As expats, we are "temporaries" in this place. Like our footprints on the sandy beach near our hut, our presence will disappear with the tide or our inevitable move. With this book, we have cast our footprints like Kindergartners placing their hands in plaster for their parents to hang on the wall imprinting this moment in time. We have published a takeaway journal of our cumulative experience as foreigners in Nigeria, and have helped provide an education for children that can change the face of a village.

About The Contributors

Moyo Adeleye, a Nigerian Travel Consultant, has lived in Nigeria all her life and loves it. She also enjoys New York City for the same hustle and bustle, but by the end of one week away, she misses the maddening, lovable Lagos. Being in Africa and being African with a rich history and culture stirs Moyo.

American **Jodi Adeyinka**, married a Nigerian, Wale, and moved to Lagos seven years ago with their son. She taught preschool and serves on the Board of Directors at AISL.

Judy Anderson takes absolutely nothing for granted since her move to Nigeria and while missing the conveniences of home, takes pleasure in exploring new cultures and places. After expat stays in England and Angola, this gal finds herself alternately grateful for all she has and embarrassed by it, but glad to be an American.

Marionette Audifferen hails from Maryland, USA. Nigeria is her first overseas assignment, where she has lived for three years with her husband and four children. She has a new dog called "Bruiser" and was the yearbook advisor for AISL.

Andrew Barton is an Australian engineer who relocated to Nigeria with his wife and two young children. In addition to his work commitments and family activities, he manages to satisfy his passion for sailing by racing in his Lightning class yacht at the Lagos Yacht Club on Saturdays.

Three years ago, American **Betsy Brock** arrived in Lagos as a newlywed, married to Randy for the second time. Look for their story in a bookstore near you.

Clare Brown has been in Nigeria for over three years with her husband and two children. British Clare has also lived three years in each of Istanbul, Moscow and Siberia. When she leaves Nigeria, she will miss the boat trip to the beach and the friends she has made here but looks forward to having distinctive seasons again.

Jack Carter first visited Lagos in 1988, but has enjoyed many visits since then. Jack has been married to Martha since meeting her in Saudi Arabia 31 years ago; they have two married children, and two grandchildren. Jack has a 1965 Shelby Cobra 427 SC, and has been active in his church wherever he lived. Growing up in Calgary, Alberta, he enjoys the snow and would like to live somewhere he could ski more.

Gail Collins, with a degree in Marketing, is new to professional writing. Her credits include personal narratives for magazines and a newspaper including: Arizona Daily Republic, Transitions Abroad, and Greenprints. She has recently returned to the States after nine years experiencing the clash and thrill of living within another culture in Europe and exploring the Nigerian frontier. She's noted that while people are vastly different, people are also quite the same, but always and in all ways, people are the story.

Kim Davis first came to Nigeria as a newlywed in 1989. Originally from New Orleans, Louisiana, she has lived overseas for 16 years starting in Nigeria then to Indonesia, Papua New Guinea, Australia and Argentina. She has now come full circle back to Nigeria with her husband, Kerry, and their two boys, Spencer and Max.

Jo Demmer, Australian, originally trained as an electrical engineer. She then studied Organisation Behaviour and reinvented herself as a Consultant working for a Career Consulting organisation.

Her latest metamorphosis is to become a trailing spouse in Nigeria, where her primary role as mother of two mischievous, young boys is entwined with working for IBSF. Her first novel is in the making.

With a degree in Geology and a Masters in Geography, **Sara Dobbs** taught at community colleges prior to arriving in Lagos five years ago with her family. Although she misses clean streets and restrooms, she will also miss Nigeria's chaos and unpredictability when she leaves. Living in Africa teaches patience and contentment.

Texan **Jared Eckert** is a ninth grader at AISL. He spent the last three years in Nigeria and will go to boarding school in Switzerland for tenth grade. A sports lover who participates in a range of sports, he is also in National Junior Honor Society and an Eagle Scout.

American **Jeff Eckert** is Jared's father and Kathy's husband. He has two other children, Ryan and Anna Grace and is heavily involved in Scouts and other fatherly duties.

Kathy Eckert, American, is a former psychotherapist and is three years into her family's first foreign assignment. With three children and a husband who commutes two minutes by foot to the office too often, Kathy holds a board position on AWC. Africa has taught her to be concerned more with who she is than with what she has.

Australian **Lindy Edwards** is an experienced expat having spent more than 17 years in Malaysia, London, USA and most recently Nigeria. An ex-teacher, Lindy is a keen golfer and enjoys volunteering at the Motherless Babies Home in Nigeria.

Charlie Fazzino is an American on his first overseas assignment in Nigeria with his wife and three boys. Working for an oil company, Charlie enjoys brewing beer, playing golf and coaching sports for his boys' sports teams as relaxation.

Shelley Fazzino, on her first stay abroad from America, finds the everyday challenges of life in Nigeria quickly bond the expat community. In addition to her own three boys, she enjoys working at the Motherless Babies Home, loving children whenever she can. Although she began volunteering there for the babies, she ended up the blessed one.

American **Mike Garbarini** has been tripping out to Nigeria for 19 years and just about everywhere else in the world his oil company works doing technical computing. Though he misses his wife, kids and pillow-top therapeutic mattress while away, the challenges of operating in developing countries has taught him that what is designed in the luxury of the US still has to work in the real world.

US born **Bob Griffith** and his wife, Heidi, made Australia home after lengthy stays in Malaysia, Great Britain and Australia. An active member of The Nigerian Field Society for nearly three years and a cyclist, Bob travels extensively around Nigeria and values the patience it has given him. He still misses the cooler weather that never comes.

After 10 years in Malaysia and two years in Nigeria, **Kerri Hakala** enjoys being surrounded by a diverse group of faithful women who enrich her life. She advises others to remain open-minded about new experiences - to give and learn from other cultures - but the American gal with a great sense of humor still misses family.

Katrina Head, a first-time American expat loves the friendliness of the local people, the luxury of staff to help with her five children, and the opportunities for travel. She does miss the reality of things that work properly a majority of the time.

Stephen Head is an eighth grade student at AISL where he is involved in baseball, French, band, technology, Boy Scouts and more. Stephen embraces the world around him, observing many of the differences in culture and traditions. He has enjoyed international trips and camps in Switzerland and France. After ninth grade, he will be off to boarding school and the adventures to come.

After adopting her two children while living in Qatar, **Ilonka Hoffmanns** knows the heart of adoptive mothers. In her year in Nigeria, she worked for a Nigerian adoption agency. This experience also gave her the opportunity to foster a sick toddler for six months, a beautiful memory that will always stay with her family.

Malaysian, **Marzuki Abdul Jabar,** is a civil engineer currently working in Nigeria. He studied in America, and met his Malaysian wife in Chicago. A family man, with five children, he enjoys the challenge of work in Nigeria.

Canadian, **Les Johnson,** married Croatian, Zdenka, and besides working in the oil industry, this tenor leads his merry band serenading police roadblocks during the holidays.

Born in Singapore to Indian parents, **Dakshina Kaushish** has American citizenship. At nine years-old, she speaks Chinese, French, Hindi, Swahili and English. Her hobbies include embroidery, swimming and tennis, but she loves writing stories and poems even more than hitting a tennis ball.

Marla Kunfermann spent her childhood as an American expat in Africa. She married Ernst, from Switzerland, and they have lived in South Africa, Egypt and Sierra Leone during the Liberian War, before coming to Nigeria in 1991. On her first morning here when Marla simultaneously had coffee, water and power, she turned to Ernst and said, "Thanks for bringing me here. I'm gonna' love this place." After that, AWC saved her life with workshops, functions and friends.

Christine Laurenssen, Dutch Canadian, is a professional expat with a childhood abroad in the USA, Germany and Ireland. Christine appreciates that Africans tend to be incredibly optimistic people - in the face of hardship, they smile, laugh, joke and sing. After a year working as a Market Research Analyst in Nigeria, she has toughened for six months of overland travel in Africa with Ben Wilkins, another of our authors, in their Range Rover, Odin, before Christine begins work in Kenya.

American **Tony Marley** has spent 16 months in Nigeria with his wife and two young children and has previous expat experience in Germany, Korea, Cameroon, Liberia, Italy, Rwanda and Democractic Republic of Congo. His diverse career background includes working for the US Government as a pilot and African specialist, the United Nations and an oil company. He enjoys bicycle touring and since being in Nigeria has learnt what "unirate" means!

After seven years in Nigeria and a couple of years off for good behavior, American **Lee McKee** is soon to be reassigned, delighting in the close-knit expat community. He'll be giving up family, Wendys and deer hunting, but his friendships follow him around the world.

Australian **Richard Perry** spent 18 months in Nigeria, predominantly based in Eket. He has since returned to Australia to continue working as an engineer. His experience as an expatriate exposed him to travel, a new culture and the honour of being crowned a Junior Chief.

With two years overseas experience in China, American **Martha Peterson**, has taught for two more at AISL. Martha appreciates seeing the world through children's eyes. Their candor, curiosity and enthusiasm are refreshing in the face of conflict, angst and the confusion of the world. Daily opportunities dragging her from her comfort zone helped her conclude that - life isn't only about her, a smile is a gift, do the right thing no matter what and God holds Africa in the palm of his hand, too.

Peruvian **Orietta Sotomayor-Skarstein** is married to a Norwegian, Geir. Previously, they lived in Mexico City and Washington D.C., but were only in Nigeria for three months before she took up professional okada riding. With a Masters in Business Administration and postgraduate degree in Economics, she was a lawyer in her other life. In one year, Nigeria has broadened her view of life creating tolerance.

After 5 years at AISL, **Marilyn Thomas-Penney** loves the international community where her students are motivated and fun to teach. She has worked in Germany and the Philippines, but misses her adult daughter in Seattle, Washington.

Richard Tulloch is the Australian author of 150 episodes of the hugely successful "Bananas in Pyjamas," over 40 children's books, several plays and screenplays, one of which was nominated in

America for the coveted Hollywood "Annie" award. He travels the world entertaining students and teachers as a guest author. He recently travelled to Nigeria where he spent time with AISL and the IBSF, and he has contributed a story inspired by his time here.

American **Michelle Ukoh** is happily married to Francis, a Nigerian. They returned to Nigeria in 2002, with their two children, after nearly two decades in the US. With a background in business and education development, Michelle has been principal of a top private school in Lagos. She enjoys painting, reading, writing, traveling and volunteering. Wherever she is, she misses her family and friends on the other side of the planet.

Belgian **Els Van Limberghen** designed the entire book layout for Nigerian Gems. She has been in Nigeria with her husband and two daughters for a year and has had previous expat experience in Burundi and Rwanda. Her time in Africa has helped her to appreciate things that she used to take for granted She sees problems from a different perspective and revitalises more often.

Mary Walker, with a degree in International Studies, this American Business Development Director has been working in Nigeria for years in executive positions for a diverse range of worldwide companies.

Sophie Wells started her great international adventure in 1996 when she moved her family of three small children from Louisiana to Sumatra, Indonesia where they fell in love with the people and overseas living. They had a wild elephant in the camp, were evacuated for four months due to severe smoke and drove jeeps whose keys fell out of the ignition around corners, but kept on running. They are hooked on this wild life and have learned that home really is where the heart is.

Tiffani Wetherbee first came from the States to Africa as a child because her father was Superintendent of AISL. She returned for visits during her parents' second assignment in Lagos and was hired on to teach in 1996. During her time in Nigeria, she has been involved in photography and music.

Ben Wilkins has a diverse background working in telecommunications, riding motorbikes and writing as a freelance journalist. He drove from London to Nigeria (except for the water parts) and is now on the way to Kenya, via South Africa. Originally from the UK, Ben has become the trailing spouse of Christine Laurenssen, who is also a contributor to the book.

Julia Yeoh, an Australian mother of three has taught in public schools and spends her leisure time reading and writing. After three years in Lagos, she has looked at life from both sides now, from up and down - Down Under to Asia to Africa.

Glossary

By Kerri Hakala and Co.

Nigeria's official language is English and there are three major indigenous languages: Yoruba, Hausa and Igbo. One of the fun aspects of communication in a multicultural society is uncovering the idiosyncrasies of different English dialects - British, American and Pidgin English to mention but a few - intermingled with local languages. Listed below are the expressions used in our stories and some of our favorites.

AISL: American International School, Lagos.

AWC: American Women's Club.

Bale: The chief of a village.

Beans cake: A Nigerian dish made from beans, pepper, tomato, onion and salt which are processed, made into patties and deep-fried.

Been to's: Refers to those who have been away and returned with all of the solutions.

Black shirt: A policeman.

Brain freeze: Of American origin, this refers to the incredible pain felt from overly enthusiastic consumption of a frozen drink.

Close for the day: Finishing work at the end of the day.

Checkpoint: Roadside police shakedown stop.

Danfo: This refers to a van-like taxi usually filled to the brim with passengers and their paraphernalia and painted with positive affirmations such as, "Don't worry be happy," "No condition is permanent" and "Jesus is my co-pilot."

Dash: To run quickly or to pay a tip for a service. The latter is the definition in Nigeria.

Disting: This thing.

Down down: A long way down.

Drop: A one way trip with a taxi.

Dunny: Australian slang for toilet.

Dunny block: An Australian public toilet block.

Ekaaro: Good morning.

Ekaabo: Welcome.

Fanny pack: American origin - pouch worn around the waist and above the fanny (bottom). Same as the Australian/British origin term bum bag.

Flashing: Revealing oneself in public, or calling a mobile phone and hanging up straight away to signal the recipient without incurring phone charges.

Fuel: pronounced FOOL, meaning petrol.

Go-slow: A Nigerian traffic jam, allowing many vendors to descend upon your vehicle in the hope of a quick sale. Also known as a "hold up."

Hard minerals: Alcoholic variety of minerals (see below).

Hello: Not a greeting, this means "I can't hear you."

Horning: To honk a car horn continuously until traffic moves (or nothing happens, which is usually the case).

How now?: How are you?

IBSF: Ishahayi Beach School Foundation

I'm coming: Means I'll be back.

I need to ease myself: What you would do upon a visit to the "White House" (see below).

It's paining me: I feel pain.

Kobo: Nigerian coins, no longer in circulation. Do not offer these at a Checkpoint.

Loo: Australian/British term referring to the below mentioned "White house."

Medevac'd: Medical evacuation.

Minerals: Refers to carbonated beverages, not a daily vitamin supplement. Known in British circles as a soft drink.

More grease to your elbows: May God continue to bless you.

Mr Biggs: A fast food restaurant in Nigeria, like McDonalds.

Naira: Nigerian currency. At the time of printing, rough conversions are: US$1 = 140 naira, €1 = 170 naira, £1 = 280, AU$1 = 100 naira.

Now now: Immediately.

Odabo: Goodbye.

Okada: A motorbike taxi found on every corner.

Ole: A Spanish cheer or Nigerian Thief.

On it/off it: Used as a verb to turn it on or turn it off.

Oyibo: Referring to those of a lighter complexion.

Pilot: A bus driver.

Pissed: American origin - angry or "pissed off," Australian/British origin - drunk.

Randy: This can be a person's name or a reference to someone's libido.

Rubber: Australian/British eraser. American-prophylactic.

Small small: Small denomination of money.

Something for the boys: This does not refer to a song by the USO (United Service Organization) for soldiers stationed overseas, but refers to the above definition for dash. This is often performed at a checkpoint or customs.

Steering: Driving.

Steward/Stewardess: someone employed to clean a house, iron clothes and generally keep a house in order.

Stone: Broken rock.

Take leg: Walk.

To spit the dummy: Of Australian origin, this term indicates extreme fury. If a baby spits out his/her dummy (pacifier) it is usually an indication that they are upset, so the expression is extended to people of any age.

Wahala: BIG trouble.

White house: The home of the President of the United States or the facilities, i.e. "I have to visit the White House."

Yellow fever: Not a disease but a traffic officer.

You are welcome: This is typically meant as a greeting not as a response to a "Thank You."

419: In the US this refers to a cleaning agent. In Nigeria - any type of fraud, it is derived from the Nigerian Penal Code where offence number 419 is to commit fraud.